Thailand

Thailand

Authentic regional recipes

Christine Watson

CHARTWELL
BOOKS, INC.

This edition published in 2011 by
Chartwell Books, Inc.
A division of Book Sales, Inc.
276 Fifth Avenue Suite 206
New York, New York 10001
USA

QTT.WFTH

A Quintet Book
Copyright © Quintet Publishing Limited

ISBN-13: 978-0-7858-2873-0

Cover photo © FoodPhotogr. Eising / Stockfood America

Project Editors: Joe Fullman, Martha Burley
Designer: Rod Teasdale
Art Director: Michael Charles
Managing Editor: Donna Gregory
Publisher: Mark Searle
Additional Text: Camilla Barton, Diana Craig

This book was conceived, designed, and produced by
Quintet Publishing Limited
The Old Brewery
6 Blundell Street
London N7 9BH
United Kingdom

Printed and bound in Singapore

10 9 8 7 6 5 4 3 2 1

Contents

Introduction

Thai cooking is all about harmony; achieving the perfect balance between the five flavors—sweet, sour, hot, salty, and bitter. This book contains more than a hundred recipes from all over Thailand, from rich green and red curries to hot and sour soups and spicy seafood salads. What they all have in common is an emphasis on fresh ingredients, usually cooked quickly so as to retain their zest and bite. These recipes showcase both the Thais' own culinary inventiveness and the influence of foreign cuisines. Over the centuries the country's cooks have appropriated ingredients from across Asia—fiery spices from India, noodles from China, and peanut sauces from Indonesia—which have been adapted to produce new and original recipes.

ABOVE: Flat cabbage, Indian lettuce, a-choy, and bok choy for sale at a Thai market.

LEFT: A beach restaurant on the Thai island of Koh Chang.

The regions of Thailand

ABOVE: Thailand's floating markets are among the most photographed destinations in the country. Boats laden with a wide variety of tropical fruits, flowers, and vegetables were once the mainstay of daily trading in the country.

Thailand is divided into four basic regions—north, northeast, center, and south. Though all have a shared culinary heritage, there are marked differences between the regions' cuisines. Some of these differences are purely practical. Ingredients necessarily vary from place to place according to climate and geography. In the tropical south, coconuts are a mainstay of many sauces, but they feature little in the cooler north where tomatoes are used instead. Seafood is popular in the center and south, which both have extensive coastlines, but is largely absent from the landlocked north and northeast where meat, particularly pork, beef, and chicken, is preferred.

Other differences are more subjective. Over time the peoples of the various region have developed clear preferences regarding the spice levels of their food. Northerners favor salty tastes above all others. In the northeast and south they tend to opt for hot and sour ones, while in the center sweet flavors are popular.

Foreign influence has played an important role in establishing these trends. Thailand is bordered by Burma to the west and north, Laos to the east, Cambodia to the southeast, and Malaysia to the south. All have had some degree of input into Thailand's culinary development, as have Vietnam, Indonesia and, particularly, China, which lies less than 60 miles from Thailand's northern border. It is from the Chinese that the Thais have inherited a love of noodles and the technique of cutting up their ingredients very small, so as to reduce the cooking time. As a result, few Thai dishes require the use of a knife. Instead, most meals are eaten using a fork and a spoon—with the fork used to push the food on to the spoon, the main eating implement.

One thing that does unite the country is rice, which is the basic staple of most meals, although, again, not all Thai people eat the same type of rice. In the center and south, steamed, fragrant rice—also known as jasmine rice—is preferred, while in the north and northeast sticky rice is favored, which is rolled into balls and dipped into sauces with the fingers.

There are no courses in a typical Thai meal. Rather, all the dishes—the soup, curry, salad, condiments, vegetables, and rice—are served at the same time, the idea being to ensure harmony and balance, not just within each invidual dish, but throughout the entire meal.

BURMA

LAOS

THAILAND

CAMBODIA

VIETNAM

*Mae
Hong Son
Province*

*Chiang Rai
Province*

*Phayao
Province*

*Nan
Province*

*Chiang Mai
Province*

*Lampang
Province*

*Lamphun
Province*

*Phrae
Province*

*Uttaradit
Province*

*Nong Khai
Province*

Nakhon Phanom Province

*Sakon
Nakhon
Province*

*Udon Thani
Province*

*Nong Bua Lam
Phu Province*

*Loei
Province*

*Tak
Province*

*Sukhothai
Province*

*Phitsanulok
Province*

*Kalasin
Province*

*Mukdahan
Province*

*Khon Kaen
Province*

*Kamphaeng
Phet Province*

*Phichit
Province*

*Phetchabun
Province*

*Chaiyaphum
Province*

*Maha
Sarakham
Province*

*Yasothon
Province*

*Amnat
Charoen
Province*

*Roi Et
Province*

*Nakhon
Sawan
Province*

*Uthai
Thani
Province*

*Chai Nat
Province*

*Lop Buri
Province*

*Nakhon
Ratchasima
Province*

*Ubon
Ratchathani
Province*

*Si Sa Ket
Province*

*Buri Ram
Province*

*Surin
Province*

Sing Bori Province

Ang Thong Province

*Kanchanaburi
Province*

*Suphan
Buri
Province*

*Saraburi
Province*

*Prachin
Buri
Province*

Nakhon Nayok Province

Nakhon Pathom Province

Nonthaburi Province

*Sa Kaeo
Province*

*Ratchaburi
Province*

*Chachoengsao
Province*

Samut Songkhram Province

*Chon Buri
Province*

*Phetchaburi
Province*

*Rayong
Province*

*Chanthaburi
Province*

*Prachuap
Khiri Khan
Province*

Samut Prakan Province

Bangkok Metropolis Province

Pathum Thani Province

Trat Province

Phra Nakhon Si Ayutthaya Province

Samut Sakhon Province

Chumpon Province

Ranong Province

*Surat
Thani
Province*

Phangnga Province

*Nakhon Si
Thammarat
Province*

*Krabi
Province*

Phuket Province

Phatthalung Province

Trang Province

Pattani Province

Satun Province

*Songkhla
Province*

Narathiwat Province

Yala Province

Northern Thailand

ABOVE: A rainbow in the mist-covered mountains of Pai, northern Thailand.

Thailand's northern region is high and mountainous with many forests. Its climate is a good deal cooler than the rest of the country, as are the tastes of its native inhabitants. Here, curries are generally mild with few spices. Salty tastes predominate, while sweet and sour ones are much less favored.

Much of the region's land is given over to agriculture, particularly in the many river valleys where flooded fields produce the sticky rice that is the region's staple food, served as an accompaniment to almost all meals, including breakfast. Elsewhere, vegetables and fruit are grown in abundance, the region's cool climes allowing for the cultivation of certain crops, such as lychees and strawberries, which do not grow well in the rest of the country and form an important part of the local economy. Each year, the people of the north hold numerous festivals in honor of its many and various fruits. Pork dishes, such as nam prik ong (minced pork with chiles and tomatoes) are also very popular in the north—more so than those of any other meat—as are dishes featuring freshriver fish, but seafood, owing to the region's distance from the sea, is rarely consumed and usually only in dried form.

The region's largest city is Chiang Mai, which was once the capital of the ancient kingdom of Lanna. Located in the lush foothills of the Himalayas, the city remained largely isolated from the rest of the country until well into the twentieth century. As a result, its people maintain a proudly independent culture. At its numerous restaurants and street stalls—only Bangkok has more—visitors can sample many of the region's distinctive dishes, such as khao soi (curried noodles), and, a specialty of the city, sai ua, or Chiang Mai sausages, which are made from preserved pork and usually served with drinks accompanied by peanuts, ginger, and chiles.

Family meals are traditionally eaten at a low table known as a kantoke, on to which are placed a succession of dishes, all eaten with sticky rice and an assortment of condiments. Today, elaborate kantoke dinners, often accompanied by traditional Lanna dancing, have become a popular tourist attraction.

RIGHT: Tea plantations in northern Thailand are popular tourist destinations.

Northeastern Thailand

ABOVE: Buddha statue in northeastern Thailand.

The I-san, as the northeast is known in Thailand, is the country's most populated region. Strangely, it's also the least fertile. The soils here are of a notoriously poor quality and much of the land is susceptible to flooding. As a result northeasterners have become masters at improvisation, making the most out of whatever they can find, and creating meals out of some rather unusual sources of protein, including geckos, grasshoppers, and snails.

Of course, the people here do also eat more traditional choices, such as pork, chicken, and beef, as well as fresh fish caught in the region's numerous rivers. These include the mighty Mekong, which marks the border between Thailand and neighboring Laos, from where various dishes have found their way into the northeastern repertoire. One of the most popular is khanom bung, a spicy crêpe eaten on festive occasions.

Whatever the ingredients, northeasterners above all like their food strongly spiced and extremely hot. This is particularly evident in the region's most famous dish, larb, a potent blend of chopped raw meat—pork, beef, chicken, or fish—and spices. Northeasterners also have a fondness for the sour taste of unripe green papaya, which features in one of the region's other well known recipes, som tam, where it is combined with chiles, fish sauce, garlic, and peanuts to form a delightful mixture of fresh and hot flavors. The northeastern version of nam pla, the fish sauce that is a mainstay ingredient throughout the country, is renowned for its strength and pungency.

As with the north, evening meals are served on a large tray on to which are placed an array of dishes—soups, curries, salads—and a wicker basket of sticky rice. Almost all meals feature this rice, which is preferred to the steamed, fragrant varieties of central and southern regions. But then, there is a plentiful supply, as it is one of the few crops suited to the northeast's flooded, poorly drained soils. In fact, the crop grows so well here that the region can sometimes support two rice harvests a year.

RIGHT: A fisherman casts his net in one of the region's numerous rivers.

Central Thailand

Home to both Bangkok, the modern Thai capital, and Ayutthaya, the former capital, central Thailand has perhaps the richest heritage of any of the country's regions. Sometimes known as the "heart" of Thailand, it was the development of rice production in the region's vast central plain that powered the expansion of the Thai state from the thirteenth century onward. It is still the country's primary rice basket, although today its fertile soils also produce a wealth of fresh fruit and vegetables. Fish and seafood, caught by an army of fishing boats scouring the Gulf of Thailand, are also popular.

In central Thailand, high and low cuisine exist in perfect harmony. At one end of the scale are the elaborate fruit and vegetable carvings that adorn many tables, a continuation of a tradition first established by cooks preparing meals for the royal family at Bangkok's Grand Palace. At the other is an abundance of simple Thai street food with Bangkok, in particular, home to a plethora of stalls selling cheap bowls of noodles, Thai-style omelets, and sizzling seafood fritters.

Many of Thailand's best known dishes, including green and red curries, and the hot and sour soups known as tom yum, originated in central Thailand, from where they have spread all over the globe. This is also where many of the signature Thai seasonings—garlic, ginger, black pepper, and chile—were first used. As influential as the region has been, however, it's never been averse to seeking inspiration from elsewhere. As the center of the country's economy, it has long acted as a magnet for migrants from other regions (and beyond) who have brought with them their own culinary traditions to add to the general pot. Indeed, the tastes of the people of the central region, who prefer their food mildly spiced with a hint of sweetness, can, along with their fondness for noodles (eaten in greater volume here than anywhere else in the country), probably be traced back to the influence of the Chinese who boast one of the region's largest immigrant populations.

Southern Thailand

ABOVE: Fresh fish drying out in the sun is a common sight on the beautiful beaches of southern Thailand.

Thailand's southern region consists of a long, narrow peninsula of land and several islands, the largest and most famous of which is the popular holiday destination of Phuket—although, today, Phuket is actually linked to the mainland by a bridge. With so many of the region's settlements lying on or near the coast, the people have become experts in harvesting the bounty of the sea, with more fish and seafood eaten here than in any other region. This is prepared in a variety of ways. Broiling is perhaps the most popular option, but fish stir-fries and salads are also widely eaten, as is fish curry, the recipe for which has been derived from neighboring Malaysia.

One of the region's other mainstays, satay and peanut sauce, is also of foreign origin, having traveled to Thailand, via Malaysia, from Indonesia. Meat is perhaps less popular than in other regions, partly as a result of the wealth of fish alternatives and partly because of the influence of the many Muslim communities living in the southern end of the region for whom the eating of pork is forbidden. However, massaman curry, a Muslim dish made of beef, peanuts, cardamom, tamarind juice, and coconut milk, is another mainstay of southern Thai restaurant menus.

The south enjoys Thailand's warmest, lushest climate, providing the perfect growing conditions for coconuts, which crop up in all manner of local recipes. The fruit's milk and cream form the basis of many curries, its oil is used for frying, and the dried, grated flesh is employed as a sort of all-purpose condiment to enhance everything from salads and soups to desserts.

Despite their fondness for coconut and the many other tropical fruits that grow in such abundance here, southern Thais are by no means sweet-toothed. In fact they are renowned for producing the hottest curries in the whole country. Southern Thai cooks like to use a lot of spices and produce fiery recipes that will test the fortitude of even the most iron-tongued of travelers.

RIGHT ABOVE: The island of Kho Phi Phi at sunset.
RIGHT BELOW: The islands in the Andaman Sea, to the southeast of Thailand, have a lush and green terrain.

ABOVE: Stir-frying is one of the most popular methods of cooking in Thailand.

Techniques and equipment used in Thai cooking

The best Thai cooking does not depend on precise quantities or strictly adhered-to recipes but is traditionally a more inventive process, with cooks using the finest of whatever ingredients are in season or close to hand. The result is an imaginative, extremely varied cuisine, consisting of composite dishes made up of an assortment of many different ingredients.

In the Thai kitchen, much of the work goes into the initial preparation of the ingredients. Meat and vegetables are cut up into small pieces so that they will cook quickly and evenly when stir-fried—one of the most popular methods of cooking. Smaller pieces also mean more surface area to coat with spices and other flavorings, which makes for a tastier dish. Another reason why ingredients are cut into bite-sized pieces is that knives were not traditionally used at the table. Diners could not cut their food up and ate instead with their fingers—perhaps scooping handfuls from a banana-leaf "bowl"—so the pieces had to be of manageable size.

For stir-frying, deep-frying, and other methods of cooking, a wok is essential—no Thai kitchen would be without one. Both skillet and saucepan rolled into one, this vital piece of equipment should ideally be made of stainless steel, as this heats quickly and evenly. A good spatula, either stainless steel or wood, is also necessary for stirring and turning the food as it cooks. Frying in a wok is best done over a gas flame as the heat is more instant and controllable than on an electric stove. As well as being stir-fried, strips or small pieces of meat may also be blanched or braised, for serving with noodles, or skewered and broiled, as in satay.

A traditional clay pot—available in Asian stores—is another useful piece of equipment in the Thai kitchen. Topped with a lid, this heats slowly and holds the heat well, and may be used for making soups and sauces.

As rice is such a staple in the Thai diet, great care is taken in cooking it. Depending on the variety, it will either be rinsed thoroughly or soaked for several hours to remove excess starch. The traditional method for cooking rice is to steam it, wrapped in cheesecloth, in a bamboo or reed basket over a container of boiling water. Modern

LEFT: A mortar and pestle is useful to make red chile paste—a key ingredient in many Thai recipes.

technology has come to the cook's aid, and there are now electric rice steamers that make the job foolproof. After steaming, the rice could be chilled overnight for additional frying the following day. Note that care must be taken to chill the rice quickly after first cooking, as *bacillus cereus,* a bacteria that can cause food poisoning, can withstand the boiling process and will start to germinate at room temperature. To be safe, always serve rice as soon as it has been cooked, or cool leftover rice as soon as possible and store in a fridge for no more than a day.

Although a food processor now tackles many of the jobs in the Thai kitchen, some dishes demand a mortar and pestle. A heavy stone one is a good all-round tool, used for anything from making curry paste to pounding garlic. Where a lighter touch is required—for example, for bruising papaya for green papaya salad—a traditional clay mortar and pestle is a better choice.

ABOVE: *Kaffir lime leaves are widely used in Thai cooking for their unmistakably citrus scent and flavor.*

Key ingredients of the Thai kitchen

Thai cooks have many ingredients at their disposal in their search for the right balance of the five flavors—salty, sweet, sour, bitter, and hot. Perhaps the saltiest of all Thai ingredients is nam pla. Made by fermenting anchovies in brine, then drawing off the liquid, this thin, brown, fishy sauce is a culinary essential. Sweetness may come from the natural sugars in foods, but for extra sweetness—for example, in desserts—Thai cooks use coconut sugar or jaggery. Oils from the same palms are used for frying.

To add tartness to a dish, a cook might use the sour, fleshy seeds of the tamarind tree, which has become a staple of Thai cuisine since its introduction from India. Other souring agents include the leaves, peel, and zest of the kaffir lime, a tropical citrus fruit, and the more delicately flavored lemongrass, with its lemony fragrance. Herbs and green vegetables supply most of the bitter flavor in Thai food. One especially bitter food—loved by Thais but an acquired taste for Westerners—is the bitter melon.

Spices, such as chiles, supply Thai food with its hot, pungent flavors. The most commonly used chiles in Thai cuisine are from the *Capsicum annuum* species. Prik kee noo (also known as bird's eye or Thai chiles) point downward from the plant and their colors change directly from green to red. Despite their size, these peppers are surprisingly hot. Prig lang chiles are a dried variety which are largely used for curry paste. If you find it hard to get hold of Thai ones, serrano chiles are a great alternative. Found fresh or toasted, they are often used in green sauces. Another choice for Thai cuisine could be jalapeños, as they are similarly hot. Pasilla chiles (also known as black chiles) are popular in Thai cooking, and are normally found dried or powdered. Their sweet, dark, and smoky aroma lends a wonderfully rich flavor to sauces. Galangal (also known as khaa or lengkuas root), is a member of the ginger family, and imparts its fresh spiciness to seafood dishes, soups, and salads when pounded to a paste and is indispensable in Thai curries. Another culinary essential, which again found its way into Thailand via Indian cooking, is turmeric. Mild in taste but strong in color, it turns any food to which it is added a bright orangey-yellow.

Other popular flavoring ingredients include two herbs—the sweetly scented leaves of cilantro, and Thai basil, which releases its full aniseed-like flavor only when cooked. Pandanus leaf, also known as bai toey, is used to flavor desserts, being second in popularity only to jasmine.

Thais eat plenty of meat, including pork, beef, chicken, and duck. Fish and seafood are also popular, either served whole (typically broiled), as part of a curry or noodle dish, or used in such condiments as oyster sauce or shrimp paste.

As elsewhere in Asia, rice is a staple food in Thailand. Thai cooks can choose from white sticky rice, which is most common in northern and northeastern Thailand, where it replaces the plain steamed fragrant rice (also known as jasmine rice) of the central and southern regions. Rice is also used to make noodles and flour. Roti, a flat, pan-fried bread, is a Thai favorite too, especially in the Muslim south. It is usually served as a sweet snack, dripping with condensed milk or stuffed with banana, but it may be savory too.

Coarsely ground peanuts are combined with other ingredients to make dipping sauces to accompany satay (meat skewers) and fried tofu cubes. A sprinkling of ground peanuts also accompanies that popular Thai dish, pad thai.

As Thailand is not a dairy-producing country, coconut milk and cream are used instead of cow's milk to add creaminess to sauces and desserts.

RIGHT: Dried prig lang chiles are commonly used in chile paste.

ABOVE: Pad thai uses the contrasting textures of mushrooms, bean sprouts, and cilantro and marries them with sweet, sour, and salty flavored sauces. See page 64 for recipe.

Iconic Thai dishes

Pad thai

One of the country's most famous gastronomic exports, pad thai is a delicious and deceptively simple stir-fry of flat rice-stick noodles mixed with a sauce made of sugar (for sweetness), tamarind juice (for sourness), and fish sauce (for saltiness). This is then combined with a host of other ingredients, which may include eggs, chiles, bean sprouts, garlic, shallots, scallions, and ginger, plus an optional source of protein—chicken, pork, beef, shrimp, fish, tofu, etc. Ingredients and quantities change from region to region, and from kitchen to kitchen. It's up to the cook to choose which ingredients and flavors will work best together. Experience and improvisation based on what's available are the key to creating a good pad thai. It is an extremely versatile dish that works equally well as part of a main meal or as a quick snack. In Thailand it's a popular street food.

Though today synonymous with Thai cooking—the name means "Thai-fried noodles"— the dish is actually believed to be of Vietnamese origin. It was popularized in Thailand via a propoganda campaign organized by Prime Minister Luang Pibulsongram during the Second World War. Concerned that the population's growing rice consumption might have an impact on rice exports—the country's principal source of revenue—he encouraged the Thai people to swap to eating noodles by portraying pad thai as a "national" dish and the eating of it as a sign of patriotism. Pibulsongram was eventually ousted in a coup, but his culinary gift to the nation continues to thrive today.

Color-coded curries

No Thai menu would be complete without a choice of green, red, or yellow curries. Their respective colors are down to the curry paste that forms the basis of the recipe. Green curries use fresh green chiles, red curries use fresh (or, more commonly dried) red chiles, while yellow curries use either red or yellow chiles mixed with turmeric. These are blended with lemongrass, galangal, garlic, shallots, kaffir lime, cilantro, and shrimp paste to form the paste. To make the curry, the paste is fried with eggplant, shallots, Thai basil leaves, kaffir lime and some sort of meat, fish, or seafood and then cooked in coconut milk. The heat level of the curry depends on the ratio of curry paste to coconut milk. Yellow curry, most often eaten in the southern part of the country, is richer and creamier than the others, as it uses coconut cream as well as coconut milk.

Salads

Thailand is particularly renowned for its fresh salads, several of which, including som tam and yum nua, originated in the northeast, where they like their food hot and sour. Som tam is a spicy salad made with unripe green papayas that has become a nationwide favorite, sold on street stalls all over the country. Its combination of garlic, chiles, green tomatoes, green beans, shredded raw papaya, fish sauce, lime juice, and jaggery should be hot, sour, and a little salty. Simple recipes which combine mango, chicken, chile, and rice in a palette of colors and flavors are typical of the Thai cuisine. Yum nua is a spicy beef salad that uses lime juice, fish sauce, and chiles to dress tender strips of beef on a bed of cilantro, salad leaves, onion, cucumber, and tomatoes. It has been voted one of the ten most popular dishes with visitors to the country.

ABOVE: Som tam salad, with papaya and chile, is a Thai favorite. See page 109 for recipe.

ABOVE: Many areas of the country hold annual fruit festivals during May. The lychee fair in Chiang Rai includes cooking competitions, parades, and beauty contests in celebration of the fruit.

Festival foods

Sweets

The typical Thai dessert course is made up of a simple selection of fruit. Although the country does have a rich tradition of crafting elaborate sweets, known as khanom, these tend to be reserved for special occasions, such as the festival of Wan Awk Pans. This comes at the end of Vassa, a three-month period in the rainy season when Buddhist monks, and some members of the public, retreat to meditate, giving up worldy pleasures such as meat, alcohol, and sweet foods. When the three months are up, illuminated boats carry offerings of kao tum mut—sticky rice sweets wrapped in banana leaves—to the monks to celebrate (and reward) the end of their period of self-denial.

Thai sweets are not just about indulgence. Many have symbolic significance and are used in ceremonies, such as weddings, or the commemoration of a new house, to bring luck. Some of these ritual sweets are golden colored (the color is derived from egg yolk) which represents prosperity and wealth. Others have numerical significance, such as khanom chun (layered dessert), an elaborate confection made up of nine separate layers; nine being a lucky number in Thailand representing advancement and progress.

Fruit

Each year Thailand's northern district holds numerous festivals in honor of its many and various fruits, which make up one of the region's most important exports. May is the peak festival season, when the town of Fang marks the lychee harvest with parades and street fairs, while nearby San Sai holds beauty pageants and cooking competitions in honor of the mango. February sees the strawberry festival in Samoeng where a variety of strawberry-based treats—including even strawberry wine—can be bought, attracting visitors from all over Thailand and beyond.

Vegetarian festival

Perhaps the best known Thai food festival is the annual celebration of vegetarian food, or kin jay, held in early October throughout the country and across Asia. The festival originated in China and is largely observed by Thai people of Chinese descent. It supposedly commemorates the period each year, during the ninth lunar month, when people's ancestors return briefly to earth to observe the behavior of their descendents, in order to make sure they are living good lives in accordance with Buddhist teaching—which of course means refraining from eating meat. The whole thing could be seen as an exercise in "putting on a front," so as not to disappoint the visiting ancestors, but it

is nonetheless taken very seriously by many people. During the ten-day festival observers refrain from eating not just meat and fish, but any animal-derived product, including milk and eggs. Strong smelling foods, such as garlic and onions, are also off-limits.

At this time street stalls with bright red and yellow signs announcing "jay" (vegetarian food) for sale appear throughout the country. At home and at schools, soybean milk, noodles with mushrooms and tofu, plus lots of vegtables are consumed as meat and dairy subsitutes. Soy sauce is also used instead of fish sauce to create special versions of pad thai and red curry. Some households even use special kitchen utensils that have never been used to cook meat, so as to avoid the possibility of "contamination."

ABOVE: These bright Thai coconut sweets are special treats for the festive period.

CHAPTER ONE

Classic dishes

While each region of Thailand has its own distinctive cuisine, often influenced by the culinary history of its neighboring countries, there are many recipes that enjoy nationwide appeal. Regional variations do still occur, of course. The emphasis on fresh ingredients that lies at the heart of all Thai cooking means that the recipe for something as widely eaten as pad thai will change from area to area according to the availability of local produce. It is this versatility that is perhaps the greatest triumph of Thai cooking. With most meals consisting of rice or noodles, accompanied by an assortment of other dishes, it is the perfect cuisine for laying on an elaborate, multi-course banquet, or for just rustling up something quick, easy, and fresh-tasting after work.

LEFT: A floating market in Damnoen Saduak near Bangkok, Thailand. The abundance of fresh, local produce in Thailand contributes to the wonderful flavors and aromas in the cuisine.

NORTHERN THAILAND

THAILAND

NORTH EASTERN THAILAND

CENTRAL THAILAND

SOUTHERN THAILAND

Fish sauce with chiles

Ingredients

4 fl. oz fish sauce

10 fresh small green and red chiles, sliced into small circles

1 tsp sliced shallot

¼ tsp jaggery (use soft brown sugar if you can't easily get hold of jaggery)

1 tbsp lime or lemon juice

Makes about 6 fl. oz

*K*nown as nam pla prik, this simple spicy sauce is found on tables throughout Thailand and is used to add both spiciness and saltiness to dishes. The fish sauce on which it is based is usually made from small fish, such as anchovies, which are then fermented using salt over many months to produce a rich, fragrant brew.

Mix all the ingredients together well. This is good for accompanying almost all Thai food, especially rice. Just sprinkle a little on your food to liven it up.

RIGHT: Nam pla prik is a quick and simple recipe which adds an authentic Thai feel to any noodle or rice dish.

Mango salsa

Ingredients

1 large ripe mango

1 small ripe pineapple

1 small red bell pepper, seeded and diced

4 scallions, chopped

Makes 3½ fl. oz

*S*weet, tangy mango salsa makes a great accompaniment to fish or chicken dishes, providing a nice contrast to the hot and sour flavors of much Thai cooking.

Peel the mango, remove the stone and finely dice the flesh. Cut away the skin of the pineapple, remove the central core and dice the flesh.

Place all the ingredients in a serving dish and stir gently to combine. Cover and refrigerate for 1 hour before serving.

Chicken, eggplant, and noodle broth

Ingredients

2 tbsp peanut oil

1 red bell pepper, seeded and finely chopped

2 garlic cloves, peeled and crushed

2 small white eggplants, cut into wedges

2 oz pea eggplant, removed from their stalk

2 shiitake mushrooms, quartered

1 tbsp Thai red curry paste (see page 156)

2 tbsp tomato ketchup

2 fl. oz coconut cream

3 boneless chicken breasts, cut into bite-sized pieces

12 fl. oz chicken broth

2 tbsp light soy sauce

Juice of 1 lime

1 tsp raw sugar

6 oz dried medium egg noodles, broken into short lengths

1 red chile, finely shredded

Serves 4

FAR RIGHT: This small round variety of eggplant is also known as kermit eggplant. RIGHT: Pea eggplants are also known as devil's fig, or turkey berry.

*T*hai eggplant is very different from the large purple and black-skinned varieties common in the West. This recipe uses two different types of Thai eggplant—the small round variety, which has a pale green, almost white skin, and pea eggplants, which grow in small clusters and have a sharp, slightly bitter flavor.

In a wok, heat the peanut oil and stir-fry the red bell pepper and garlic for 3–4 minutes over a medium heat until the pepper is almost tender. Add the eggplant and shiitake mushrooms and cook for a further 2 minutes.

Add the Thai red curry paste and cook for 30 seconds. Stir in the tomato ketchup and coconut cream, cook for 1 minute, and then add the chicken, broth, light soy sauce, lime juice, and sugar.

Simmer for 10 minutes. Meanwhile, cook the egg noodles in a saucepan of boiling water for 4 minutes. Drain and divide between four serving bowls. Spoon over the chicken broth and serve sprinkled with the shredded red chile.

Spiced chicken soup

*T*o save time, this recipe uses prepared satay sauce (or peanut butter) and pre-mixed Thai 7-spice seasoning, a blend of salt, chili powder, garlic, ginger, cilantro, lemon peel, and black pepper, which can be found in most supermarkets.

Heat the oil in a large pan; add the chicken and 7-spice seasoning and cook quickly until the chicken begins to brown. Stir in the lemongrass and potato, then add the stock and milk. Bring slowly to a boil, then cover and simmer for 20 minutes.

Stir in the scallions and peas. Bring the soup to a boil and continue cooking for a further 5 minutes.

Add the satay sauce or peanut butter to the soup just before serving. Remove from the heat and stir until melted. Season to taste, and then serve garnished with a spoonful of heavy cream.

Ingredients

1–2 tbsp peanut or sunflower oil

2 small, skinless, boneless chicken breasts, shredded

2 tbsp Thai 7-spice seasoning

1 stick lemongrass, finely chopped

2 medium potatoes, diced

1½ pints chicken or vegetable stock

1 pint milk

3–4 scallions, trimmed and finely sliced

3 oz frozen peas

1–2 tbsp satay sauce or peanut butter

Salt and freshly ground black pepper

1–2 tbsp heavy cream, to garnish

Serves 4

RIGHT: The multi-colored display of spices which make up the 7-spice seasoning. Each spice is readily available on the Damnoen Saduak floating markets in Thailand.

Clear soup with stuffed mushrooms

Ingredients

3 pints homemade clear stock, beef or chicken

18 small, dried shiitake mushrooms

1 small piece of winter melon

Stuffing for mushrooms:

½ lb finely ground pork with a little pork fat

2 cloves garlic, crushed

4 stems of cilantro, finely chopped with leaves
   chopped separately

Salt and freshly ground black pepper

2 tsp soy sauce

1 scallion, trimmed and chopped

6 water chestnuts, peeled and chopped

Few cilantro leaves to garnish

Serves 8

The Asian mushrooms used in this recipe are most commonly known by their Japanese name, shiitake. In Thailand they are known as hed hom or fragrant mushrooms.

Prepare the stock or use a stock cube with a little soy sauce for color. Soak the mushrooms for 30 minutes until soft. Remove the stalks and set aside.

Meanwhile prepare the stuffing for the mushrooms. Mix the pork, garlic, cilantro stems and leaves, seasoning, soy sauce, scallion, and water chestnuts together. Divide the mixture between the soaked mushrooms. Place the stuffed mushrooms in a bamboo steamer over a wok with a sheet of greaseproof paper as a lid. Cook for 20 minutes.

While the mushrooms are cooking bring the stock to the boil. Add the cubes of melon and cook until just tender.

Place the stuffed mushrooms and a few cubes of melon in each serving bowl. Pour over the soup and scatter with a few cilantro leaves.

Mini vegetable and herb rolls

*P*ad khad kow, also known as Chinese cabbage, features in many Thai recipes. When filling the rolls, it is important to remember not to pack them too tightly or they may burst open when plunged into the hot oil.

Heat 2 tablespoons of peanut oil in a wok and stir-fry the carrot, Chinese cabbage, celery, mushrooms, and garlic for 2–3 minutes over a medium heat until just softened.

Stir in the celery leaves, chives, and parsley and set aside to cool.

Lay the spring roll wrappers on a board and spoon a little of the filling onto each. Brush the edges of the wrappers with egg white and roll up from one corner to the opposite one, tucking in the sides and pressing the edges together to seal.

Heat the peanut oil to 350°F and fry the rolls in batches for about 3 minutes until golden brown. Drain on paper towel and serve hot with a dipping sauce.

Ingredients

2 tbsp peanut oil plus extra for deep-frying
3 oz grated carrot
3 oz Chinese cabbage, finely shredded
2 sticks of celery, finely diced
2 oz shiitake mushrooms, finely chopped
1 garlic clove, peeled and crushed
1 tbsp finely chopped celery leaves
1 tbsp snipped chives
1 tbsp chopped fresh parsley
5-in spring roll wrappers (squares of phyllo pastry)
1 egg white, lightly beaten

Serves 4

Spiced onions

*T*hese onions are only lightly cooked, to retain flavor and color. This makes an excellent side dish with broiled fish. Total preparation and cooking time is just 15 minutes.

Heat the oil in a large skillet or wok, then add the coriander seeds, lemongrass, and chiles. Fry quickly for 1–2 minutes.

Stir the sliced onions and the red onion into the skillet and stir-fry quickly for approximately 2–3 minutes.

Add the scallions and toss them in the juices. Heat for just a few seconds, then stir in the fish sauce. Add lime juice and salt to taste.

Serve the onions garnished with the shredded coconut and cilantro.

Ingredients

2 tbsp peanut oil
1 tbsp coriander seeds
1 stalk lemongrass
1 green and 1 red chile, seeded and finely
   chopped
2 large onions, thickly sliced
1 red onion, cut into 8 segments
10–12 scallions, cut into 2-in pieces, finely
   sliced lengthwise
2 tbsp fish sauce
Lime juice and salt to taste
Coconut and cilantro, shredded

Serves 4

Lime-marinated pork skewers

Chicken could be substituted for the pork if you prefer. When slicing the lime leaf to make the dipping sauce, use small sharp scissors or a knife—if the slices are not wafer thin they will be unpleasant to eat.

To make the dipping sauce, stir the ingredients together until the sugar dissolves. Set aside for at least 1 hour to allow the flavors to develop.

Meanwhile, prepare the skewers. Mix the garlic, lime juice, sugar, fish sauce, soy sauce, and lemongrass and ginger purées together in a bowl, stirring until the sugar dissolves.

Add the pork and stir so the cubes are well coated. Cover and leave in a cool place to marinate for 1–2 hours.

Drain the pork and carefully thread the cubes onto the skewers. Broil or barbecue the skewers for 5 minutes, turning them over once or twice and brushing with any marinade left in the bowl.

Serve the skewers hot with the dipping sauce.

Ingredients
Dipping sauce:
3 tbsp light soy sauce
1 kaffir lime leaf, very finely sliced
1 tbsp fish sauce
Juice of 1 lime
1 tsp raw sugar
1 green chile, seeded and finely sliced

Skewers:
3 large garlic cloves, peeled and crushed
Juice of 3 limes
1 tbsp granulated brown sugar
1 tbsp fish sauce
1 tbsp light soy sauce
1 tsp fresh lemongrass purée
½ tsp fresh ginger purée
1 lb lean pork steaks, cut into 1-in cubes

Serves 4

Vegetable fritters with chile relish

*T*he quantities given for the relish will make more than is needed for the recipe, but any leftover can be stored in a screw-top jar in the refrigerator for up to two weeks.

To make the chile relish, soak the red chiles in hot water for 30 minutes. Drain, cut open, and remove the seeds. Pat dry on paper towels. Heat the peanut oil to 350°F for deep-frying and fry the chiles for 2–3 minutes. Drain on paper towels. Transfer 2 tablespoons of the peanut oil to a wok and fry the green bell pepper and shallots for 5 minutes over a medium heat. Add the garlic, fry for 2 minutes and then stir in the tomatoes, green chiles, and shrimp paste.

Lower the heat and simmer gently for 30 minutes. Cool a little and then purée in a food processor with the sugar and fish sauce. Return the purée to the wok and cook very gently for about 40 minutes until dark, caramelized, and thick, stirring frequently so it does not stick to the wok and burn.

To make the fritters, mix together the snow peas, scallions, sweetcorn, green bell pepper, crunchy peanut butter, fish sauce, sugar, and mint. Stir in the flour and then the beaten egg to bind the mixture together.

Reheat the peanut oil to 350°F for deep-frying. Drop tablespoons of the mixture into the hot oil and fry for 3–4 minutes until golden brown. Drain and serve hot with a little of the chile relish. Garnish with lemon wedges and mint leaves.

Ingredients

For the chile relish:
½ oz large dried red chiles
Peanut oil for deep-frying
1 red bell pepper, seeded and chopped
4 shallots, peeled and chopped
2 garlic cloves, peeled and finely chopped
8 oz chopped tomatoes
1 tsp shrimp paste
2 tbsp raw sugar
4 fl. oz fish sauce

For the fritters:
8 snow peas, finely chopped
2 scallions, finely chopped
4 oz sweetcorn kernels
½ green bell pepper, finely chopped
1 tbsp crunchy peanut butter
1 tbsp fish sauce
1 tsp white sugar
1 tbsp chopped fresh mint
3 oz all-purpose flour
1 egg, beaten

To garnish:
Lemon wedges
Mint leaves

Serves 4–6

Stir-fried greens

*P*ossibly the fastest dish to cook in Thailand, this is properly made with the water plant variously known as swamp cabbage, water cabbage, morning glory, ung choy, and water convolvulus.

Heat the oil in a wok or skillet until it is very hot.

Carefully add all the ingredients at once (watch for splattering), and quickly stir-fry for about 2 minutes.

Serve accompanied by steamed rice, or chicken, eggplant, and noodle broth (page 31).

Ingredients
3 tbsp peanut or corn oil
11 oz swamp cabbage leaves and stems, cut
    into 4-in lengths
4 fl. oz chicken broth
2 tbsp marinated soybeans
1 tbsp garlic, chopped

Serves 4–6

Thai hors d'oeuvre

A *hard-to-find treat in Thailand, but always enjoyed. The Thais use fresh tree and vine leaves, but lettuce does just as well. You may need to soak the leaves in hot water for 2–3 minutes to aid their flexibility.*

To make the sauce, preheat the oven to 350°F. Roast the coconut, shrimp paste, galangal, and shallots for 5 minutes until fragrant. Leave to cool. Place with the peanuts, shrimp, and root ginger in a blender or food processor and blend together into a fine mixture.

Transfer the mixture to a heavy-bottomed pan with the sugar and water, mix well and bring to a boil. Simmer until it is reduced to about 5 fl. oz. Remove from the heat and leave to cool.

To serve, first pour the sauce into a serving bowl and arrange all the ingredients in separate piles on a platter or in small bowls.

When everything is prepared, take a vine or lettuce leaf and place a small amount of each of the garnishes in the middle. Top with a spoonful of sauce and fold up into a little package. Repeat until you have the desired number of packages.

Ingredients
5 tbsp unsweetened grated coconut
3 tbsp shallots, finely diced
3 tbsp lime juice
3 tbsp fresh root ginger, diced
3 tbsp dried shrimp, chopped
3 tbsp unsalted roasted peanuts
2 tsp fresh small green chiles, chopped
1 bunch of edible vine leaves or lettuce

For the sauce:
2 tbsp unsweetened grated coconut
½ tbsp shrimp paste
½ tsp galangal, sliced
½ tsp sliced shallot
3 tbsp unsalted peanuts, chopped
2 tbsp dried shrimp, chopped
1 tsp fresh root ginger, sliced
8 oz jaggery (or soft brown sugar)
6 fl. oz water

Serves 6–8

Thai vegetables

For this recipe you'll require a pressure cooker and a lot of care. Thai chiles (also known as bird's eye or prik kee noo chiles) are very hot indeed. Use sparingly unless you know that you can take the heat. Wear rubber gloves when handling.

Heat the oil in the open cooker and sauté the garlic, lemongrass, root ginger, chiles, and cinnamon stick for 2 minutes. Add the vegetables and sauté for 1 minute.

Pour in the coconut milk with 3 fl. oz of boiling water then close the lid and bring to 15 lb pressure. Cook for 1 minute then depressurize quickly and discard the lemongrass and cinnamon. Season and serve sprinkled with the chopped cilantro.

For really crisp vegetables, bring to pressure then remove from the heat and depressurize quickly. For soft vegetables, pressure cook for 2 minutes.

Ingredients

1 tbsp sunflower oil

2–3 garlic cloves, peeled and crushed

2 lemongrass stalks (outer leaves discarded), bruised

1 small piece fresh root ginger, peeled and finely grated

1–2 Thai chiles (see page 20) or green jalapeño chiles, seeded and chopped

1 cinnamon stick, bruised

6 oz broccoli florets

6 oz cauliflower florets

2 carrots, peeled and chopped

1 large zucchini, trimmed and cut into thick slices

4 oz green beans, trimmed and halved

6 fl. oz coconut milk

Salt and freshly ground black pepper

1 tbsp chopped fresh cilantro

Serves 4

Chicken, mango, and rice salad

Ingredients

6 fl. oz water

1 tbsp fish sauce

½ tsp shrimp paste

1 tbsp raw sugar

1 tsp fresh lemongrass purée

Zest and juice of 1 lime, finely grated

1 tbsp Thai basil, finely torn

1 lb cooked rice, cooled

1 green mango, peeled, flesh cut away from the stone, and thinly sliced

1 lb cooked chicken meat, sliced

4 oz beansprouts

4 oz green beans, cooked

1 slice of pineapple, cut into small pieces

1 green chile, finely sliced

Serves 4

*T*hai salads are hot and sour and use lots of fresh vegetables and herbs such as basil, chives, and mint. Instead of chicken, this recipe can also be made with mixed seafood such as scallops, squid, and shrimp.

Place the water in a saucepan with the fish sauce, shrimp paste, sugar, lemongrass purée, lime zest, and juice and bring to a boil. Simmer for 2 minutes, then remove from the heat and stir in the basil. Set aside to cool.

Divide the rice between four cups or small basins, pressing down so the rice is quite tightly packed, then turn out onto four serving plates.

Arrange the mango, chicken, beansprouts, green beans, and pineapple around the rice and scatter over the green chile. Spoon over a little of the dressing and serve the remainder separately.

Beef and arugula salad

*A*dd extra chili powder if you like your dishes spicy, but only add half if you prefer your salads to be cool.

Mix together the chili powder, ground coriander, black pepper, and ginger. Roll the fillet in the spice mix until coated.

Heat the peanut oil in a heavy skillet and seal the fillet on all sides until well browned. Allow to cool, then wrap tightly in plastic wrap and place in the freezer for 30 minutes, to make it easier to slice later.

Remove the fillet from the freezer, unwrap, and slice as thinly as possible.

Mix together the lemongrass, cilantro, mint, fish sauce, rice vinegar, superfine sugar, and red chile.

Once defrosted, arrange the fillet slices on a serving dish so that they overlap. Pile the arugula and chard leaves in the center and spoon over the dressing. Scatter over the cashews, and serve garnished with the scallions.

Ingredients

½ tsp chili powder
1 tsp ground coriander
½ tsp ground black pepper
Pinch of ground ginger
1 lb fillet of beef in
   one piece
1 tbsp peanut oil
½ tsp lemongrass purée
1 tbsp roughly chopped cilantro
1 tbsp chopped mint leaves
1 tbsp fish sauce
2 tbsp rice vinegar
1 tsp superfine sugar
1 red chile, seeded and finely chopped
4 oz arugula leaves
1 oz red chard leaves
2 tbsp chopped cashews, lightly toasted
2 scallions, shredded

Serves 4

Green bean salad with shallot croutons

Ingredients

For the chile paste:

4 oz shallots, finely chopped
1 tbsp chopped garlic
4 anchovy fillets
8 fl. oz water
2 tbsp sliced fresh ginger
2 tbsp sliced lemongrass
1 dried red chile, seeded
1 tsp dried shrimp paste (optional)
Pinch of salt

For the salad:

8 oz green beans
3 tbsp grated unsweetened coconut, fresh or
    desiccated
4 fl. oz peanut oil
6 garlic cloves, sliced ⅛-in thick lengthwise
2 fl. oz fresh lime juice
2 fl. oz unsweetened coconut milk
1 tbsp red chile paste (see above)
1 tbsp Thai fish sauce
1 tbsp sugar
12 whole radicchio leaves
2 serrano chiles (see page 20), preferably
    1 red and 1 green, seeded and chopped
Cilantro sprigs, to garnish

For the shallot croutons:

Peanut oil
4 medium shallots, sliced ⅛-in thick

Serves 4–6

*F*inely diced chicken breast or prawns, or a combination, can be added to this salad to make a hearty lunchtime or supper meal.

Mix the chile paste ingredients together in a wok or pan, then cook over a medium heat for 1 minute. Allow to cool, before processing to a paste in a food processor.

Blanch the beans in a saucepan of boiling, salted water for about 3 minutes, until tender but still crisp. Drain and rinse under cold running water. Cut the beans into bite-sized pieces and set aside.

Heat a dry wok or small skillet, add the grated coconut, and toss gently for about 1 minute, until golden. Transfer the coconut to a plate.

Pour the peanut oil into the wok and heat to 375°F using a deep-fat thermometer. Remove the wok from the heat, add the garlic slices, and stir until golden and crisp. Transfer the garlic to paper towel to drain.

In a bowl, whisk together the lime juice and coconut milk, then whisk in, one ingredient at a time, the chile paste, fish sauce, and sugar. Set aside. Make the shallot croutons by heating the oil in a wok to 375°F (again, measure using a deep-fat thermometer). Remove the pan from the heat, add the shallots and stir for about 3 minutes, until the shallots are crisp and golden. Transfer to paper towel to drain. The shallots can be refrigerated, covered, for up to a week, but should then be lightly toasted on a baking sheet in the oven before using.

Arrange the radicchio leaves on a platter or individual plates. In a large bowl, combine the beans, the toasted coconut, and the garlic slices. Pour the mixture of lime juice, coconut milk, chile paste, fish sauce, and sugar over the beans, coconut, and garlic. Gently fold in the serrano chiles and serve garnished with cilantro sprigs.

Rice salad with roasted coconut

This is a classic "leftover" dish which can be made with rice from the night before. For health and safety reasons, do not use rice that has been chilled for more than 24 hours.

Sprinkle the grated coconut on a baking sheet and place in an oven set at 350°F. Roast the coconut for 5–8 minutes until brown and crisp.

Put all the sauce ingredients in a pan, boil for 5 minutes, remove from the heat, and then strain.

Place the rice in half-cup molds or large ramekins, press and invert onto a large serving platter. Arrange the rest of the raw ingredients around the edge of the rice in separate piles. To eat, spoon some rice onto individual plates and take a little of each ingredient to mix with the rice according to taste. Spoon the sauce over the top.

Ingredients

For the salad:
4 oz unsweetened grated coconut
8 oz cooked rice, cooled
1 small pomelo or grapefruit, shredded
2 oz dried shrimp, chopped
2 oz bean sprouts
2 oz lemongrass, finely sliced
1 oz string beans, sliced
2 dried red chiles, pounded
1 tbsp kaffir lime leaf, finely shredded

For the sauce:
8 fl. oz water
2 tbsp anchovies, chopped
1 tbsp jaggery (or soft brown sugar)
2 kaffir lime leaves, torn into small pieces
¼ tsp lemongrass, sliced

Serves 4

Noodle and napa cabbage salad in a peanut dressing

Ingredients

For the salad:

1 lb thin noodles

8 oz snow peas

1 red bell pepper, cut into strips

1 medium cucumber, thinly sliced

4 scallions, cut diagonally into thin slices

4 oz napa cabbage (also known as Chinese) leaves, shredded

For the peanut dressing:

4 oz creamy peanut butter

4 fl. oz plain non-fat yogurt

1 tbsp soy sauce

1 garlic clove

2 tbsp dark sesame oil

3 tbsp chopped fresh cilantro

2 tbsp rice wine vinegar

Serves 4

*T*he variety of textures in this dish is typical of Thai cuisine. The combination of soft noodles and crunchy vegetables in a nutty dressing ensures an exciting eating experience.

Cook the noodles in a large pan of boiling water according to the packet directions, until they are tender. Drain well, transfer to a large serving bowl, and set aside. (If you are working ahead of time, toss with 1 tablespoon vegetable oil.)

Trim the stalk ends from the snow peas and blanch in boiling water for about 1 minute. Drain well and rinse in cold water—they should be bright green in color. Add the snow peas, red bell pepper, cucumber, and scallions to the noodles. Add the napa cabbage and toss again and serve.

To make the dressing, simply work the yogurt into the peanut butter, then add all the other ingredients and mix well.

Chicken fried rice with onion and garlic

*O*ne of the basic standard Thai dishes, this always tastes best with rice from the day before—and is also much easier to cook if the rice has been chilled in the fridge overnight. For health and safety reasons, be cautious and do not use rice which has been chilled for over 24 hours. In place of chicken, pork or shrimp are also commonly used.

Heat the oil in a wok or pan, add the chicken and garlic and mix well over the heat for 1 minute.

Add the onion and cook for another minute.

Break in the eggs, mix very well and then stir in the rice until it is piping hot.

Serve immediately accompanied by cucumber slices, tomato wedges, chopped scallion, and nam pla prik (fish sauce with chiles, see page 28).

Ingredients

3 tbsp peanut or corn oil

7 oz skinless, boneless chicken breasts, cut lengthwise into ½-in thick slices

1 tbsp chopped garlic

1 medium-sized onion, sliced

2 eggs

16 oz cooked rice, chilled

½ cucumber, sliced

1 tomato, cut into 8 wedges

1 scallion, chopped

5 tsp fish sauce with chiles (see page 28)

Serves 4

Curried fried rice with green haricot beans

*T*his recipe is all about balance—finding the perfect ratio of salty and sweet flavors to compliment the tender meats and crunchy vegetables. It's also a great way of using up any leftover rice and cooked meats. Galangal (Thai ginger or khaa root) adds a stronger flavor to the curry paste.

Cut the meats into fine slices, but leave the shrimp whole. Set the rice on one side. Wash, prepare and blanch the beans.

Use a mortar and pestle or food processor to mix up the chiles, shallots, garlic, lemongrass, galangal, and the cilantro stems and peel. If using the chili powder add it to these pounded ingredients. Heat the oil and fry this paste until it gives off a fragrant aroma.

Add the cooked meats and fry for around 1 minute. Add the rice, stirring all the time until the rice and the other ingredients are well mixed together. Add more oil if necessary to prevent the rice from sticking.

Season with salt, fish sauce, and sugar to taste. Finally add the green beans. Serve garnished with cilantro leaves.

Ingredients
½ lb cooked meats, chicken, pork, and shrimp
1 lb cold, cooked long-grain rice
4 oz green haricot beans, or long beans, cut into 2-in lengths and blanched
Fish sauce and sugar to taste

For the curry paste:
3–5 dried red chiles, seeded, or 1–2 tsp chili powder
6 shallots, finely chopped
2 cloves garlic, chopped
2 stems of lemongrass, use bottom part of bulb, sliced
½ in galangal, finely sliced
4 stems of cilantro, chopped, with the leaves reserved for garnish
A little grated lime peel
6–8 tbsp vegetable oil

Serves 4–6

Chicken with Thai basil

Ingredients

1 lb boneless, skinless chicken breasts, cubed

4 tbsp fish sauce

3 tbsp vegetable or sunflower oil

4 garlic cloves, peeled and sliced

2–4 red chiles, seeded and chopped

2 tsp dark soy sauce

½ tsp sugar

15 Thai basil leaves

Serves 4

*T*hai basil, known as bai jorapa or holy basil, has an aniseed flavor quite different from the sweet basil used in much Mediterranean cookery. Bunches of it can be found in many Asian food stores. Best served with steaming hot jasmine rice, this dish is popular throughout Southeast Asia.

Marinate the chicken in three tablespoons of the fish sauce, and set aside for at least 30 minutes.

Heat the oil in a skillet and fry the garlic and chiles until golden, which should take about about 2–3 minutes.

Add the chicken and fry until it starts to turn brown, which again should take around 2–3 minutes.

Add the remaining fish sauce, soy sauce, and sugar. Stir for about 3–4 minutes or until well cooked.

Finally stir in the basil leaves, cook for a further 1 minute and serve immediately.

LEFT: Soy sauce is popular throughout Asia, and styles vary from country to country. Apart from the ubiquitous soy sauce, soy beans are made into a variety of stir-fry and cooking sauces. In Thai cuisine, a thin soy sauce works best, or black bean and yellow bean varieties.

Barbecue chicken with chile vinegar sauce

*I*f *it is not the right time of year for a barbecue, the chicken can be cooked under a conventional broiler or in a ridged cooker-top pan. Serve with sticky rice (page 86) or fragrant rice (page 128).*

Place the chicken breasts side by side in a shallow dish. Mix together the light soy sauce, fish sauce, brown sugar, garlic, chile purée, and peanut oil. Keep stirring until the sugar has dissolved.

Pour the soy sauce mixture over the chicken, turning the breasts over so that they are well coated. Cover and leave to marinate in a cool place for at least 2 hours.

To make the sauce, heat the rice vinegar and sugar gently in a small pan until the sugar dissolves. Simmer for 2 minutes, stirring regularly, then remove from the heat and stir in the ginger purée, red chile, and light soy sauce. Allow to cool.

Lift the chicken pieces from the marinade and barbecue them for 10–15 minutes or until cooked through, brushing regularly with any marinade left behind in the dish. Cut each chicken breast into 3 or 4 thick slices and serve with the sauce spooned over.

Ingredients
For the chicken:
4 skinless, boneless chicken breasts
2 tbsp light soy sauce
1 tbsp fish sauce
1 tsp granulated brown sugar
2 garlic cloves, peeled and crushed
1 tsp fresh chile purée
1 tbsp peanut oil

For the sauce:
6 tbsp rice vinegar
2 tbsp raw sugar
½ tsp fresh ginger purée
1 red chile, seeded and finely chopped
1 tbsp light soy sauce

Serves 4

RIGHT: In Bangkok, a street vendor barbecues quick, fresh dishes.

Chicken and pineapple with three-flavor sauce

Ingredients

For the three-flavor sauce:

2 tbsp peanut oil

2 cloves garlic, peeled and minced

1 tsp fresh ginger purée

1 medium red chile, seeded and chopped

2 shallots, peeled and finely chopped

2 tbsp jaggery (or soft brown sugar)

1 tsp tamarind paste

1 tbsp fish sauce

Juice of 3 limes

2 tbsp peanut oil

6 boneless chicken thighs, skinned and cut
   into bite-sized pieces

4 scallions, trimmed and sliced

1 slice pineapple, cut into small pieces

5 fl. oz chicken stock

4 kaffir lime leaves, cut into wafer thin strips

Serves 4

*T*his dish is known in Thailand as gai tod saporot. It features a
   sauce that crops up in dishes all over the country, offering a
balance of sour, sweet, and salty flavors. Although it contains some
chile, the sauce is not particularly hot. If most diners prefer not to
have the chile content increased, lovers of hot food can add extra
fire by adding nam prik (chile sauce) as a condiment. Replace the
chicken with raw shrimp if you prefer.

To make the sauce, heat the oil in a wok and fry the garlic, ginger, purée, chile, and
shallots over a low heat for 3 minutes. Crumble in the sugar and cook until it caramelizes
to a rich, red brown. Add the tamarind paste, fish sauce, and lime juice and remove
from the heat.

Heat the oil in a skillet and stir-fry the chicken in two batches for 1–2 minutes over a
brisk heat. Remove and set aside.

Add the scallions and pineapple to the skillet and stir-fry for 1 minute. Transfer the
scallions and pineapple to the three-flavor sauce in the wok, stir in the stock, and
bring to a simmer. Lower the heat, add the chicken and lime leaves, and cook gently for
10 minutes.

Serve with noodles as well as a green vegetable, such as bok choy or snow peas.

Chicken pad thai

*C*hicken pad thai is one of Thailand's most popular and best known noodle dishes. It requires a type of medium flat rice-stick noodle known as sen lek in Thai. A vegetarian version of this dish—minus the chicken and substituting vegetable for chicken stock—loses none of the taste, as it can easily be bulked out with additional tofu (bean curd). See page 164 for an alternative version of pad thai with shrimp.

Soak the noodles in hot water for 7–10 minutes, drain, and set aside.

Mix the sauce ingredients together in a pan and boil until reduced to about two-thirds of a cup. Set aside to cool.

Drain the noodles. Heat the oil in a wok or skillet until it just starts to smoke, and then stir-fry the chicken for 2–3 minutes. Add the chopped ginger, garlic, and chile, and stir-fry for 1 minute. Add the tofu and stir-fry for 1 minute, then break in the eggs. Stir-fry for 1 minute before adding the noodles and stock.

When the noodles are soft, add the remaining ingredients and the sauce, and stir-fry for 2 minutes. Garnish with the lemon, the cucumber slices, and the cilantro leaves, and serve immediately.

Ingredients

For the noodles:

11 oz dried medium flat rice-stick noodles

3 tbsp peanut or corn oil

6 oz skinless, boneless chicken breast, finely
sliced

½ inch fresh root ginger, finely chopped

2 cloves garlic, finely chopped

1 red bird's eye chile, chopped

4 oz tofu (also known as bean curd), diced

4 eggs

2 fl. oz chicken stock

3 tbsp sliced shallots

3 tbsp dried shrimp, chopped

3 oz unsalted peanuts, chopped

4 scallions, sliced

15 oz bean sprouts

Slices of lemon, to garnish

Slices of cucumber, to garnish

Fresh cilantro leaves, to garnish

For the sauce:

8 fl. oz water

4 fl. oz tamarind juice

2 oz sugar

1 tbsp light soy sauce

Serves 6

Fried rice noodles with chiles and vegetables

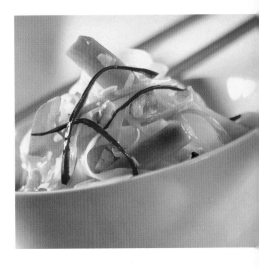

Using four red chiles, this is a fiery, hot dish. But it also has its more delicate flavors, particularly the lemongrass—a staple of many Thai dishes—which gives it a pleasant, tangy perfume.

Cook the noodles in lightly salted boiling water for 3 minutes. Drain, and plunge into cold water, then drain again and reserve.

Heat the oil in a wok or large skillet and stir-fry the lemongrass and ginger for 2 minutes. Discard the lemongrass and ginger, reserving the oil in the pan.

Add the onion, garlic, and chiles, and stir-fry for 2 minutes. Add the red pepper and cook for a further 2 minutes. Add the remaining vegetables and stir-fry for a further 2 minutes.

Finally add the reserved noodles and cashew nuts with the soy sauce, orange juice, and honey. Stir-fry for 1 minute. Add the sesame oil and quickly stir-fry for a final 30 seconds. Serve immediately.

Ingredients

6 oz dried medium rice-stick noodles

2 tbsp sunflower oil

2 lemongrass stalks, outer leaves removed
   and chopped

1-in piece fresh root ginger, peeled and grated

1 red onion, cut into thin wedges

2 garlic cloves, crushed

4 red bird's eye chiles, seeded and sliced

1 red bell pepper, seeded and cut into
   matchsticks

4 oz carrot, very thinly sliced

4 oz zucchini, trimmed and sliced

3 oz snow peas, trimmed and cut diagonally in
   half

6 scallions, trimmed and diagonally sliced

4 oz cashew nuts

2 tbsp soy sauce

Juice 1 orange

1 tsp clear honey

1 tbsp sesame oil

Serves 4

Spicy rice-stick noodles with chicken

*A*uthentic Thai spicy noodles are very, very hot. If you don't think your taste buds can take it, simply reduce the number of green chiles that you use. However, if you feel like increasing the spices, you can add more green chile, if you dare.

If you use fresh noodles, just rinse with warm water. Soak dried rice noodles in warm water for 2–5 minutes, or according to the instructions on the package. Rinse, and drain.

Heat 3 tablespoons of the oil in a wok or skillet until very hot. Stir-fry the garlic and green chile for 30 seconds, then add the chicken and fry for about 3 minutes more.

Add the green beans, mustard greens or spinach, and baby corn, stirring for 1–2 minutes. Add the remaining oil and the rice noodles, and stir. Then add the fish sauce, both soy sauces, and sugar, and stir well.

Garnish with the tomatoes, and serve immediately.

Ingredients

2 lb fresh flat rice noodles or 10 oz dried rice-stick noodles

5 tbsp vegetable oil

2 cloves garlic, finely chopped

4–6 small green chiles, chopped

½ lb boneless chicken breasts, sliced into bite-sized pieces

4 oz frozen green beans, halved

¼ lb mustard greens or fresh spinach

16 canned or fresh baby corn, each cut diagonally into 3 pieces

4 tbsp fish sauce

3 tbsp dark soy sauce

2 tbsp light soy sauce

1 tbsp jaggery (or soft brown sugar)

2 small tomatoes, halved

Serves 4

Rice-stick noodles with pork and shrimp

Ingredients

10 oz dried rice-stick noodles

5 tbsp vegetable oil

2 cloves garlic, finely chopped

3 shallots, chopped

½ lb lean pork, sliced into small pieces

¼ lb peeled shrimp

4–6 small green chiles, chopped

10 oz bean sprouts

3 stalks celery, cut diagonally into bite-sized
  pieces

2 eggs, beaten

2½ tbsp jaggery (or soft brown sugar)

3½ tbsp tomato ketchup

6 tbsp fish sauce

½ fl. oz freshly squeezed lemon juice

Cilantro leaves, chopped

Serves 4

*T*his dish contains three of the main foundations of Thai flavoring: garlic, shallots, and chiles. Thai garlic tends to be small compared to its western counterpart, so if the cloves you have are on the large side, use just one.

Soak the rice-stick noodles in warm water for 2–5 minutes, or according to the instructions on the package. Rinse, and drain.

Heat 3 tablespoons of the oil in a wok or skillet, and stir-fry the garlic and shallots for 30 seconds. Add the pork and fry for about 3 minutes. Add the shrimp and green chiles, stirring for another minute, then add the bean sprouts and celery, and fry for another 2 minutes.

Make a well in the center, then pour in the eggs and scramble quickly. Add the remaining oil and the rice-stick noodles, then stir. Add the sugar, tomato ketchup, fish sauce, and lemon juice, and stir well.

Divide the noodles into four bowls, and garnish with chopped cilantro.

Crisp fried rice vermicelli

*T*he thin, fried vermicelli rice noodles, known as sen mee in Thai, give this dish a delicious crisp texture. The noodles are sold dried in rolls and bound together in bundles. They need to be soaked briefly in cold water to soften them, but they must then be dried thoroughly before frying or they will spit dangerously when added to the hot oil. It is also important to heat the oil to the correct temperature or the vermicelli will be tough and chewy rather than crisp. If you don't have a cooking thermometer, place the handle of a wooden spoon in the hot oil; when bubbles form around it, the oil is ready.

Finely chop the chicken breast, cut the cooked pork into fine slices and set aside with the shrimp. Fry the shallots and garlic in hot oil in a wok; do not color. Add the chicken and stir for 3–4 minutes, then stir in the pork and shrimp. Turn the ingredients all the time.

Add the tofu (bean curd) cubes and salted soybeans and cook for 2–3 minutes. Then add the beaten eggs little by little, stirring throughout and adding extra oil if necessary to the sauce.

At this stage stir in the vinegar, confectioners' sugar, and fish sauce. Toss in the pan for 1–2 minutes, then check the flavor. It should have a sweet, salty taste. Set aside.

Heat oil to 375°F in a large pan and deep-fry the noodles for just a few seconds. This is best done in several stages in a frying basket or wok. The noodles will become puffy and crisp. Remove them from the fat. Drain and keep warm.

Just before serving, put half the sauce and a sprinkling of the chili powder in a large wok or pan with half the noodles. Toss together without breaking up the noodles too much. Repeat this tossing procedure with the remaining sauce, chile, and noodles.

Pile onto a large serving platter and garnish attractively with chiles, cilantro, garlic, and lime rind or grapefruit shreds. Arrange the scallions all around the base.

Ingredients

For the sauce:
4 oz raw skinless, boneless chicken breast
2 oz cooked pork
4 oz cooked shrimp, shelled
Oil for frying
6 shallots, chopped
2 cloves garlic, crushed
1 square tofu (bean curd), yellow or white, cut into neat cubes
½ a 12-oz can salted soybeans
4 beaten eggs
1 fl. oz cider or wine vinegar
1–2 tbsp confectioners' sugar
Fish sauce to taste

For the noodles:
Fat for deep-frying
12 oz rice vermicelli
¼ tsp chili powder

Garnish:
2–3 red chiles, deseeded and finely sliced
Fresh cilantro leaves
Pickled garlic or fried garlic flakes, chopped
Rind of lime or strip of grapefruit peel, cut into fine shreds
6 oz scallions, tails removed for best effect

Serves 6–8

Crispy fried rice vermicelli with garlic, fish sauce, and lime stir-fry sauce

Ingredients

For the garlic, fish sauce, and lime
   stir-fry sauce:
1 tsp fresh garlic purée
Juice of 1 lime
1 tsp soft brown sugar
2 red chiles, seeded and finely chopped
3 tbsp fish sauce
1 tbsp rice vinegar

7 oz rice vermicelli
Peanut oil for deep-frying
6 oz lean pork, cut into small pieces
2 skinless, boneless chicken breasts, cut into
   small pieces
1 red bell pepper, seeded and chopped
4 oz bean sprouts
2 large eggs, beaten
2 tbsp fresh cilantro

Serves 4

*T*he three flavors of garlic, fish sauce, and lime are the triumvirate of Thai cuisine. Here they combine to form the basis of a hot, salty, sweet and sour sauce for stir-frying pork, chicken, and mixed vegetables. This dish is known as mee krob in Thailand. As with most stir-fries, you may vary the ingredients according to their availability. Shrimp, diced tofu, ground turkey, and other vegetables, such as carrots, baby corn, and scallions, can also be used.

To make the sauce, simply mix the ingredients together, stirring until the sugar dissolves.

Snip the vermicelli into short lengths and soak briefly in cold water to soften. Dry thoroughly on paper towel.

Heat the oil for deep-frying in a wok to 375°F, add the vermicelli a little at a time and fry until they are lightly golden and crisp. Drain on paper towel.

Pour off most of the oil from the wok, leaving about 2 tablespoons. Reheat, add the pork, and stir-fry for 2 minutes over brisk heat. Add the chicken and stir-fry for 3 minutes. Remove and set aside.

Add the red bell pepper, the bean sprouts, and the snow peas and stir-fry for 3 minutes. Return the pork and chicken to the wok and add the sauce. Toss for 1 minute, then add the eggs and stir until they have set.

Add the noodles and herbs and toss together over the heat until well mixed. Garnish with fresh cilantro and serve at once before the noodles have started to soften.

Chicken with peppers and bean-thread noodles

*B*ean-thread noodles—also known as cellophane noodles, glass noodles, and woon sen in Thai—are a type of thin, dried transparent noodle made from mung beans. In this recipe they are accompanied by a tasty stir-fry that uses fresh kaffir lime leaves. If you have difficulty finding fresh ones, most supermarkets sell dried ones, or you could just leave them out.

Soak the bean-thread noodles in boiling water for 4 minutes, then drain and set aside until required.

Use a sharp knife to slice the peppers and carrots into thin strips, and then grate the ginger, lemongrass, and garlic.

Cut the chicken into strips. Heat a wok until hot then add the oil. Heat for 30 seconds, then stir-fry the chile, lime leaves, ginger, lemongrass, and garlic for 1 minute. Add the chicken strips and continue to stir-fry for 3 minutes, or until browned.

Add the pepper and carrot and stir-fry for 4 minutes. Add the noodles and stir-fry for 2 minutes. Pour in the soy sauce and fish sauce and stir-fry for another 2 minutes, or until the chicken is completely cooked through. Sprinkle with the chopped cilantro and serve immediately.

Ingredients

8 oz bean-thread noodles

1 red pepper, seeded

1 yellow pepper, seeded

1 green pepper. seeded

2 carrots

2-in piece fresh root ginger

2 lemongrass stalks, outer leaves discarded

2–4 cloves garlic

2 x 5-oz skinless, boneless chicken breasts

2 tbsp groundnut oil

1–2 Thai chiles (see page 20), seeded and chopped

2 kaffir lime leaves

2 tbsp light soy sauce

1 tbsp fish sauce

2 tbsp chopped cilantro

Serves 4

Fried bean-thread noodles with tofu

Ingredients

For the noodles:

½ lb bean-thread noodles

4 tbsp vegetable oil

10 oz tofu (bean curd), diced

3 cloves garlic, finely chopped

16 oz bean sprouts

4 oz frozen green beans, halved

2 scallions, chopped

2 tbsp roast peanuts, crushed

2 tbsp dried shrimp, chopped

3–5 small green chiles, chopped

2½ tbsp jaggery (or soft brown sugar)

6 tbsp fish sauce

4 fl. oz freshly squeezed lemon juice

For the garnish:

2 tbsp crisp onions

Cilantro leaves

1 medium red chile, sliced

4 slices of lime

Serves 4

*T*ofu, or bean curd, is a favorite constituent of Thai cooking. Note that it is always best to use all of your tofu in one go as it quickly deteriorates, even if refrigerated.

Soak the bean-thread noodles in boiling water for 5 minutes. Rinse under cold water, and drain. Heat half the oil in a wok or skillet, and fry the tofu until golden brown. Drain on paper towel.

Add the remaining oil to wok, then fry the garlic for about 30 seconds. Add the bean sprouts, green beans, and scallions, and stir well.

Add the bean-thread noodles, tofu, crushed peanuts, dried shrimp, and green chile, then stir. Season with the sugar, fish sauce, and lemon juice, stirring again.

Divide the noodles onto four plates. Sprinkle with the crisp onions, cilantro leaves, and red chile, and garnish with the lime slices. Serve at once.

LEFT: The Grand Palace in Bangkok is beautifully adorned with brightly colored statues. It is the gem of Bangkok's impressive collection of temples and palaces.

Spicy egg noodles with beef and vegetables

*B*a mee, or Thai egg noodles, are the basis of this dish. They have a distinctive yellow color in contrast to the more commonly used white rice noodles. The shrimp paste used in this recipe is highly pungent, but do not let the odor put you off. Wise Thai cooks make sure their kitchen is well ventilated while they are cooking.

In a large pan, bring a quantity of water to a boil, add the egg noodles and cook for 4 minutes. Rinse under cold water and drain.

Heat the oil in a wok or skillet, and stir-fry the red chiles, garlic, and shrimp paste, if using. Add the beef and fry for 2–3 minutes or until cooked.

Stir in each ingredient as you add the onion, green chiles, bean sprouts, and spinach. Season to taste with the salt and pepper.

Add the noodles, sprinkle over both soy sauces, and mix well. Divide the noodles among four plates and garnish with cilantro leaves and lime wedges. Serve immediately.

Ingredients

10 oz dried, medium egg noodles

3 tbsp vegetable oil

2–3 small dried red chiles, soaked in hot water, then ground

2 cloves garlic, finely chopped

1 tsp dried shrimp paste (optional)

10 oz round steak, thinly sliced

1 medium onion, thinly sliced

2 green chiles, chopped

7 oz bean sprouts

4 oz fresh spinach

Salt and black pepper, freshly ground

3 tbsp dark soy sauce and light soy sauce

Cilantro leaves

4 lime wedges

Serves 4

Egg noodles with tofu and vegetables

*T*his is a partnership of flavors that is classic in Thai cooking. Here the tofu and vegetables are served with a distinctive, aromatic sauce.

Cook the noodles in a pan of boiling water for 4 minutes, then drain. Blanch the peas in another pan of boiling water for 2 minutes before draining.

Heat the oil in a wok or skillet, add the garlic, shallots, and chiles, and stir-fry for 2 minutes. Add the tofu and stir-fry for 2 minutes more.

Add the bean sprouts and carrot and stir-fry for 2 minutes. Add the noodles, fish sauce, lime juice, and sugar. Stir-fry over a high heat for 2–3 minutes. Before serving, sprinkle the cilantro and peanuts over the noodles and garnish with lime wedges.

Ingredients

10 oz dried medium egg noodles

4 oz sugar snap peas, cut into halves

2 tbsp sunflower oil

2 cloves garlic, minced

2 shallots, sliced

3 small green chiles, chopped

10 oz firm tofu, diced into ½-in cubes

4 oz bean sprouts, rinsed

1 carrot, shredded

2 tbsp fish sauce

2 tbsp fresh lime juice

1 tbsp brown sugar

3 tbsp chopped fresh cilantro

2 tbsp roasted peanuts, chopped

4 wedges lime, for garnish

Serves 4

Mango sorbet

A water ice made with ripe mangoes, this sorbet needs beating every hour until it is frozen, to break up the large ice crystals, but it should still retain an icy, grainy texture. You can subsitute any really ripe soft fruit for the mango.

Make a syrup by bringing the water and sugar to a boil, stirring to help dissolve the sugar. Simmer for a few minutes, then remove from the heat and allow to cool.

Remove the mangoes' skin and rind, cut into pieces, and feed through an electric strainer to obtain a thick purée. Then mix the purée with the syrup and lemon juice.

If you are using an ice cream machine, follow the manufacturer's instructions, adding the egg white for the last 5 minutes of the churning.

If you do not have an ice cream machine, add the egg whites to the mango purée, then turn into a shallow plastic container. Open-freeze the sorbet, removing from the freezer every hour and beating to break up the ice crystals.

When almost frozen, but still liquid in the center, tip the mixture into a mixing bowl and beat until free of ice crystals.

Before serving, place the container in the refrigerator for 1 hour to soften the sorbet and make it easier to scoop out.

Ingredients

8 fl. oz water

3¼ oz superfine sugar

2 large ripe mangoes, peeled, pitted, and cubed

Juice of a lemon

1 large egg white, lightly beaten

Serves 4

Lemongrass and lime mousse

Ingredients

2 lemongrass stalks, tough outer layers removed

2 fl. oz water

2 eggs, separated

3½ oz superfine sugar

Grated zest of 1 lime, plus more for garnishing

Juice of 1½ limes

10 fl. oz heavy cream

½ oz powdered gelatin

Serves 4

*T*his mousse has a wonderfully delicate flavor and provides a light, clean finish to a meal.

Using a rolling pin, thoroughly crush the lemongrass to release its flavor. Place in a saucepan, cover with water, and simmer for 10 minutes. Allow to cool in the pan.

Meanwhile, using a food mixer, whisk the egg yolk with the sugar on the fastest speed setting until you have a thick, pale mixture. Add the lime zest, lime juice, and cream and briefly whisk again.

When cool, remove the lemongrass from the pan and discard. Reheat until almost boiling, then sprinkle the gelatin over the liquid, remove from the heat, and stir until the gelatin has dissolved completely. Allow to cool slightly and then, with the mixer running at medium speed, slowly pour the gelatin onto the egg mixture until thoroughly combined. Transfer to another bowl and set aside.

Wash the whisk and mixing bowl thoroughly before whisking the egg whites until firm. Add to the mixture in the reserved bowl and fold in until just combined.

Pour into four individual serving dishes and refrigerate for 1–2 hours. Sprinkle with lime zest to serve.

LEFT: The bold beauty of Canna Lilies are a common sight in Thailand. According to Thai mythology, Canna Lilies are guarded by deities who bless them with peace and harmony.

CHAPTER TWO

Northern Thailand

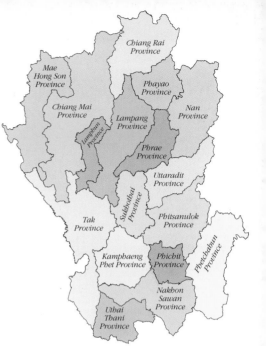

Chiang Rai
Province

Mae
Hong Son
Province

Phayao
Province

Chiang Mai
Province

Nan
Province

Lampang
Province

Lamphun
Province

Phrae
Province

Uttaradit
Province

Sukhothai
Province

Phitsanulok
Province

Tak
Province

Phetchabun
Province

Kamphaeng
Phet Province

Phichit
Province

Nakhon
Sawan
Province

Uthai
Thani
Province

This is a mountainous region dotted with many thick forests. The soils here are extremely fertile, producing a wide range of vegetables which find their way into many local dishes. Far from the coast, the people here enjoy little fresh seafood. Pork, chicken, and beef are the main sources of protein, often cooked in mild curry sauces that bear the culinary imprint of Burma to the north. Indian ingredients, such as ginger, turmeric, and tamarind, are also popular. Coconut is used less widely than in the tropical south. Instead, tomatoes, which elsewhere feature mainly as a salad vegetable, form the basis of many sauces. Almost all meals are accompanied by sticky rice, which is rolled into balls and dipped into sauces using the fingers.

LEFT: Despite the distance from the coast, dishes like fish cakes are a seafood favorite in Chiang Mai.

Sticky rice

*I*n northern and northeastern Thailand almost all meals are
accompanied by a special type of rice known as sticky or
"glutinous" rice. True to its name, the rice's high starch content
makes the grains stick together when cooked. Thai people use their
fingers to roll the rice into balls and dip it into sauces. Note that for
the best results, the rice grains need first to be soaked in water for
several hours.

Ingredients
8 oz sticky rice

Serves 4

Put the sticky rice in a bowl and pour over cold water to cover by 2 inches. Leave the rice to soak for at least 4 hours or overnight.

Rinse the rice 3 times in lukewarm water and drain very well.

Transfer the rice to a steamer lined with cheesecloth. Be careful to spread the grains out.

Steam for 20–25 minutes until the rice is tender. Do not let the boiling water touch the bottom of the rice.

The rice should be taken off the heat and allowed to rest for about 10 minutes before it is served.

Spicy meat and tomato dip

Ingredients

6 dried red chiles, chopped
3 tbsp chopped shallots
1 tbsp sliced lemongrass
1 tbsp chopped garlic
2 tsp shrimp paste
2 tsp salt
2 tbsp peanut or corn oil
4 oz ground pork
8 cherry tomatoes, diced
4 fl. oz water
Lemon juice, to taste
Fish sauce, to taste (optional)
Sugar, to taste (optional)
1 oz chopped cilantro
2 oz pork rinds, to serve

Serves 4–6

This relatively mild dip, known as nam prik ong in Thai, is heavily influenced by the cooking of neighboring Burma. In typical northern Thai fashion, guests eat from the bowl in which it is served, scooping it up with the accompanying pork rinds, vegetables, or sticky rice.

Pound the chiles, shallots, lemongrass, garlic, shrimp paste, and salt together with a mortar and pestle or in a food mixer until fine.

Heat the oil in a wok or pan and add the chile mixture, the pork, and the tomatoes. Cook for about 15 minutes, or until the sauce has thickened. Add the water and cook again for 10 minutes until thick.

Adjust the seasoning to taste with lemon juice, and the fish sauce or sugar. Garnish with the cilantro.

Serve accompanied by raw or slightly cooked vegetables, sticky rice, and if you can buy them, crisp pork rinds.

Northern Thai soup

*I*n the landlocked north, dried shrimp, sold in markets throughout the region, is often used instead of fresh varieties. The shrimp, fish sauce, and tamarind juice give this dish a salty, tart taste.

Soak the shrimp in cold water for 5 minutes. Drain and leave to dry on a paper towel.

Boil the water in a pan, add the chicken, and cook for 7–10 minutes until well cooked. Remove and cut across into thin slices.

Using the same cooking water, add the pork, preserved cabbage, onion, and fish sauce. Boil and then add the rest of the ingredients.

Boil again before pouring into bowls. Serve accompanied by sticky rice (see page 86).

Ingredients
16 fl. oz water
6 oz skinless, boneless chicken breasts
10 oz ground pork
1 tbsp preserved cabbage
4 oz onion, sliced
2 tbsp fish sauce
½ oz dried large shrimp
½ oz spinach leaf
2 tbsp tamarind juice

Serves 4–6

Raw beef salad

The peoples of both northern and northeastern Thailand have a special fondness for raw meat dishes. This recipe is extremely easy and quick to prepare. For the best results use high quality beef which should be chopped up only at the last minute.

Finely chop the beef sirloin using a sharp knife. Cut the beef liver into thin slices. Transfer all the chopped meat to a mixing bowl.

Add the rest of the ingredients—the beef blood, mint leaves, scallions, lime juice, fish sauce, and chili powder—to the mixing bowl. Using your fingers, carefully mix the ingredients together.

Portion the salad out onto serving plates, and serve accompanied by raw swamp cabbage, raw cabbage wedges, fresh basil, onion rings, and sticky rice (see page 86).

Ingredients

7 oz very fresh lean beef sirloin
2 oz beef liver
2 fl. oz very fresh beef blood
1 oz mint leaves
3 tbsp finely sliced scallion
3 tbsp lime or lemon juice
½ tbsp fish sauce
1½ tsp chili powder
1 red onion, chopped into rings

Serves 6

Northern Thai chicken curry with red chiles

A spicy chicken curry with no curry powder—instead northern Thai cooks use chopped red chiles to add fire to this dish. The chicken is cooked with its skin and bones to add extra flavor.

Heat the oil in a pan, add the chile paste and fry over a medium heat for 1 minute. Add the chicken pieces, fry until they begin to brown, then add the water and the remaining ingredients.

Simmer until the chicken is tender and the curry reduced to about half its original volume. This should take around 20 minutes.

Serve accompanied by rice.

Ingredients
Peanut or corn oil
2 oz chile paste (see page 51)
1 lb chicken (with skin and bone), cut into
   small pieces through the bones
2½ pints water
4 kaffir lime leaves, quartered
2 stalks of lemongrass, halved
1 tbsp fish sauce

Serves 4–6

Northern Thai pork curry

T
his dish originally came from across the Burmese border, as shown by the use of tamarind and turmeric. The jaggery adds a hint of sweetness, which nicely offsets the tart flavor of this curry.

Pound the lemongrass, galangal, shrimp paste, and chiles to a smooth paste with a mortar and pestle or blend in a food mixer, then mix with the pork

Transfer the paste to a saucepan with the water, turmeric, and soy sauce. Bring to a boil and cook until tender, which should take about 15 minutes, then add the rest of the ingredients. Boil again for 5–8 minutes and remove from the heat.

Taste and season with fish sauce if desired.

Ingredients
4 stalks lemongrass, chopped
1 tbsp chopped galangal
1 tbsp shrimp paste
4 dried red chiles, chopped
2¼ lb pork belly, cut into ½-in thick strips
1¼ pints cold water
1 tbsp turmeric
1 tsp soy sauce
10 shallots, sliced
2 oz jaggery (or soft brown sugar)
2 oz fresh root ginger, chopped and pounded
2 fl. oz tamarind juice
2 tbsp garlic, chopped
½ tbsp soybeans
Fish sauce, to taste (optional)

Serves 6

Curried noodles

Ingredients

2½ pints thin coconut milk

4 tbsp red chile paste (see page 51)

11 oz skinless, boneless chicken breasts, cut
   lengthwise into ½-in thick slices

1 tbsp light soy sauce

1 tbsp dark soy sauce

2 tsp salt

7 oz dried or 15 oz fresh egg noodles

Peanut or corn oil for frying

Serves 4–6

*T*his is a favorite lunch in Chiang Mai and other towns in
northern Thailand. The curry ingredients give away its Indian
antecedents, but khao soi, as it is known, has arrived via Burma, in
particular from Shan State. The crispy noodles are added at the last
minute to stop them from going soggy, while the various condiments
give each diner some control over the dish's flavor.

Heat ½ pint of the coconut milk in a pan or wok, add the chile paste, and fry for
2 minutes, then add the chicken and soy sauces. Stir-fry for 3 minutes, then add the
remaining coconut milk and bring to a boil for 3 minutes. Add the salt and remove from
the heat.

Fry 4 oz of the noodles in hot oil until crisp. Remove and drain well. Boil the remaining
noodles in water until firm but tender, then drain.

Place the boiled noodles in individual serving bowls, and pour the chicken mixture on
top. Garnish with the fried noodles.

Serve accompanied by bowls of diced shallots, pickled cabbage, and chili powder.

Chiang Mai noodles with chicken

This Thai specialty is also known as khao soi, and is originally from the Chiang Mai area in the northwestern part of Thailand. Ensure you use fresh egg noodles—or soak dried noodles for 20 minutes before you start cooking.

Heat the peanut oil in a wok. Add the red curry paste and the chili powder. Cook gently for 2–3 minutes.

Add ¼ pint coconut milk and the chicken. Continue to stir-fry for 2–3 minutes.

Turn the heat down and add chicken stock, fish sauce, and the rest of the coconut milk. While the chicken is cooking, boil the noodles and drain. Place the noodles in a large bowl and when the chicken is cooked pour over the noodles.

Garnish with chopped shallots, scallions, and cilantro. Serve with lime wedges.

Ingredients

1 tbsp peanut oil
2 tbsp red curry paste (see page 156)
2 tbsp chili powder
1¼ pints coconut milk
10 oz chicken, chopped
1¼ pints chicken stock
1 tbsp fish sauce
½ lb egg noodles
4 oz shallots, chopped
A few sprigs of cilantro
2 scallions, chopped
1 lime, cut in wedges

Serves 4

Chiang Mai sausages

Ingredients

1 tbsp fish sauce
2 cloves garlic
2 tbsp cilantro leaves
1 tbsp lemongrass purée
1 tbsp galangal (or ginger) purée
2 tbsp red curry paste (see page 156)
2 red chiles, seeded and roughly chopped
4 kaffir lime leaves
1 lb ground pork
30-in sausage casing
Sprig of Thai basil

Makes 6

Sai ua is the name given to the spicy sausages from Chiang Mai sold on street stalls throughout the city. They come in a variety of shapes and sizes, from small bite-sized balls to long spirals filled with enough meat to feed an entire family.

Place the fish sauce, garlic, cilantro leaves, lemongrass, and galangal purée, curry paste, chiles, and lime leaves in a mortar and pestle, or food mixer, and blend to a fine paste.

Place the pork in a mixing bowl. Add the paste and thoroughly mix together. Leave to marinate in the fridge for at least 2 hours or overnight.

Use your fingers to push the mixture into the sausage casing. Make each sausage around 4 inches long and tie off the ends.

Fry or broil the sausages and serve with sticky rice (see page 86) and a sprig of Thai basil.

LEFT: Doi Suthep temple in Chiang Mai. Doi Suthep mountain is one of the most revered religious destinations in Thailand.

Flat breads

*B*read is uncharacteristic of Thai cooking. This recipe found its way into the north of the country from India, via Burma. These rotis are mainly eaten as dessert snacks rather than as part of a main meal.

Mix all the ingredients, except for the oil, together well in a bowl—if the mixture is too wet to shape, add a little more flour. Shape the dough into bite-sized balls and flatten them into 4-inch circles by throwing them onto a lightly floured table surface—be careful to throw them quite horizontal.

Heat just enough oil to cover the bottom of a skillet. Place the flattened dough balls in the pan and cook over medium heat for about 3–4 minutes on each side, until lightly browned. Drain on paper towel and repeat.

Three delicious ways of serving the flat breads are: to place an egg on top of each browned roti, flipping it over to cook the egg and rolling it up to eat (perhaps with coffee); to sprinkle them with sugar and condensed milk; or to spread them with butter.

Ingredients

6 oz all-purpose flour

2 fl. oz water

1 tbsp butter, softened

1 egg

¼ tsp salt

Peanut or corn oil for frying

Makes 7–8

Sticky rice with mangoes

Ingredients
14 oz sticky rice (see page 86)
14 fl. oz thin coconut milk
2 oz sugar
½ tsp salt
½ tsp cornstarch
2 ripe mangoes, peeled and sliced
Mint leaves, to decorate

Serves 6

A simple but always successful dessert, this works because of the delicious contrast between the sticky, tangy rice and the sweet, juicy, yellow Thai mango.

Soak the rice in water for 4 hours, rinse well three times in lukewarm water and drain very well. Transfer the drained rice to a steamer lined with cheesecloth. Be careful to spread the grains out. Cover and steam for about 25–30 minutes until fairly soft.

Mix 12 fl. oz of the coconut milk with the sugar and half of the salt. Stir in the rice and mix well.

Mix the remaining coconut milk with the remaining salt and the cornstarch together in a small saucepan, bring to a boil, simmer for 2 minutes, and cool.

Place the sticky rice onto serving plates, spoon the coconut sauce over the top, and arrange the mango slices around the edges. Decorate with the mint leaves.

CHAPTER THREE

Northeastern Thailand

Of all the people in Thailand, those of the northeast, or I-san region, enjoy perhaps the most varied and interesting diet. A combination of poor soil and frequent floods has led the locals to acquire tastes for some very unusual ingredients. Red ant salad, fried grasshoppers, and lizard curry are all dishes that can be enjoyed by curious visitors. It is probably this resourceful approach to cooking that accounts for the strength of the local sauces. Here people like their food spicy, as shown in two of the region's most famous dishes: larb, a strong, sour salad, traditionally made with raw meat and blood; and som-tam, an extremely spicy green papaya salad. As in northern Thailand, most meals are accompanied by sticky rice.

LEFT: A candle ceremony in Uborachathani, northeastern Thailand.

Green papaya salad with lemongrass, cilantro, and ginger dressing

*S*alads are an important part of Thai cuisine, particularly in the northeast where green papaya salads are extremely popular. A "green" papaya is one that is slightly under-ripe so that the salad is not too sweet or soft. Only the freshest ingredients should be used, which is why in Thailand most people shop early at their local market before the sun has had a chance to wilt the delicate produce. The papaya should be prepared just before serving so that it does not lose its firm texture. This particular recipe, which features pork and mango, is known as yam mamuang.

To make the dressing, simply mix all the ingredients together in a bowl.

Heat the oil in a skillet, add the shallot, and fry for 5 minutes. Stir in the garlic, pork, and ground coriander and stir over a fairly brisk heat for a couple of minutes until the pork starts to brown. Add the soy sauce and cook, stirring occasionally, until the sauce has been absorbed by the meat and the pork is quite dry. Remove from the heat and set aside.

Using a mortar and pestle, pound the papaya with 2 tablespoons of the dressing or blend to a coarse purée in a food processor. Spoon into a serving dish, top with the warm pork, mango, and tomatoes, and pour over the remaining dressing. Serve garnished with fresh cilantro.

Ingredients

For the dressing:
½ tsp fresh lemongrass purée
1 tsp fresh ginger purée
1 tbsp chopped fresh cilantro
2 tbsp fish sauce
1 tbsp chopped mint
Juice of 2 limes
1 tsp soft light brown sugar
2 red chiles, seeded and finely chopped

2 tbsp peanut oil
1 shallot, peeled and finely chopped
1 garlic clove, peeled and minced
9 oz finely ground pork
1 tsp ground coriander
2 tbsp light soy sauce
9 oz unripe green papaya, seeded, peeled, and cut into matchsticks
1 mango, peeled and chopped
4 cherry tomatoes, halved or quartered
Fresh cilantro

Serves 4

Spicy green papaya and vegetable salad

Ingredients

1 medium green papaya, peeled and
    quartered, seeds removed

½ cucumber, cut in half lengthwise, seeds
    removed

2 carrots, peeled

2 tbsp chopped unsalted and roasted peanuts

2 garlic cloves, finely chopped

3–5 green chiles, to taste

1 tbsp sugar

1½ tbsp lime juice

1 tbsp fish sauce

15 cooked shrimp (optional)

4 fine green beans, topped, tailed and broken
    into 1-in pieces

4 cherry tomatoes, halved

1 tbsp finely chopped flat-leaf parsley

3 mint leaves, finely chopped

Serves 2

*T*his salad, known as som tam, is bursting with invigorating flavors and fragrances. If you can't find green, under-ripe papaya (the inside will be white), leave the papaya out altogether and use extra cucumber (seeds removed) and carrot (peeled), or a mixture of both, instead. A ripe papaya will simply turn to mush used in this recipe.

First, grate the papaya and vegetables, then cover and set aside.

Prepare the dressing. In a food mixer, blend half the peanuts, the garlic, and the chiles together for about 3 minutes. Then, with the mixer set on a slow speed, add the remaining ingredients, ending with the grated vegetables. Mix everything together until thoroughly combined.

Serve on a large platter with the remaining peanuts sprinkled over the top.

Crab, pomelo, and rice noodle salad

A mixture of seafood, green papaya, and pomelos, this salad takes just 15 minutes to prepare and makes a light but satisfying lunch.

Cook the rice noodles according to the package instructions and drain.

Mix together the lime juice, red chile, fish sauce, and sugar, stirring until the sugar dissolves. Toss with the warm noodles and set them aside to cool.

Cut the cucumber into long strips using a vegetable peeler. Peel the pomelo, pull away the pith, and break the flesh into bite-sized segments.

Add the cucumber, pomelo, grated green papaya, and crab claws to the noodles and toss lightly together.

Transfer to a serving dish and serve with extra lime wedges to squeeze over.

Ingredients
9 oz dried medium rice-stick noodles
Juice of 2 limes
1 red chile, seeded and very thinly
    sliced
2 tbsp fish sauce
1 tsp superfine sugar
½ cucumber
1 pomelo
5 oz green papaya, peeled and grated
12 crab claws
Lime wedges

Serves 4

Fried catfish spicy salad

Ingredients

2 whole catfish (1 lb 2 oz each), cleaned and gutted

Peanut or corn oil for deep-frying

1 green unripe mango, cut into matchsticks

4 tbsp unsalted roasted peanuts

7 fresh small green chiles, chopped

3 tbsp shallots, sliced

3 tbsp fish sauce

2 tbsp cilantro leaves and stems, cut into 1-in pieces

Serves 4–6

*T*his crisp salad is often served as a snack to accompany drinks—an important and distinct category of dish in Thailand, where drinking tends to be separated from the eating of the main meal.

Steam the catfish for 15 minutes until well cooked. Remove all the skin and bones and chop into slices.

Heat the oil in a wok or pan until hot, about 350°F, sprinkle in the chopped fish and fry until light brown and crispy, which should take around 3–5 minutes. Remove with a slotted spoon or strainer and drain well.

Mix all the remaining ingredients except the cilantro with the fish. Place the salad on plates, garnish with cilantro, and serve accompanied by sticky rice or bean sprout salad.

Grilled beef salad with fish sauce, herb, and lime dressing

*T*his spicy broiled beef salad, known as yum nua, is enlivened by the addition of a hot and sour dressing. Because the beef in yum nua is only lightly cooked, it must be as tender as possible, so sirloin, rump, and fillet steak are the best cuts to use. Trim any fat from the steak before broiling, and after broiling allow it to stand for 10 minutes so it is easier to carve into very thin slices. A cast-iron ridged grill pan is recommended because it can be heated to a sufficiently high temperature to seal the meat and ensure that it stays tender, but a conventional broiler could be used as well.

To make the dressing, place the ingredients in a covered container and shake well, or whisk together in a bowl until combined and the sugar has dissolved.

Brush the steak with the oil and cook in a grill pan over a high heat until well-browned but still pink in the center. Alternatively, broil the meat under high heat and set aside for 10 minutes, reserving any juices that have come out of the meat.

Arrange the lettuce, arugula, onion, tomato slices, scallions, and cucumber on a serving dish. With a sharp knife, slice the steak as thinly as possible and mix the slices in with the salad leaves and vegetables. Whisk any meat juices into the dressing and spoon this over the salad.

Toss lightly and serve sprinkled with chopped chile.

Ingredients
For the dressing:
2 tbsp fish sauce
2 cloves garlic, peeled and minced
1 tbsp rice vinegar
Juice of 1 lime
1 tsp soft brown sugar
2 tbsp chopped fresh cilantro
2 tbsp chopped mint

For the salad:
1 lb fillet or thick sirloin steak in one piece
2 tbsp peanut oil
3½ oz mixed lettuce and arugula leaves
1 small onion, peeled and finely sliced
2 scallions, sliced
2 tomatoes, cut into thin wedges
½ cucumber, cut into thin strips
1 red chile, seeded and sliced

Serves 6

Spiced ground chicken

*O*ne of the special characteristics of this northeastern meat *dish is the addition of uncooked sticky rice, which is first roasted (either in an oven or in a dry wok) until golden and then pounded in a mortar. It adds a slightly nutty flavor and gives the dish more body.*

Cook the chicken in a nonstick pan over a low heat for 10 minutes—do not add water or oil. When cooked, transfer to a bowl and mix well with all the remaining ingredients, except the mint.

Check the seasoning, and add more lemon juice, fish sauce, or chile if necessary. Sprinkle the mint over the top to garnish.

Serve accompanied by raw cabbage leaves, scallions, and raw string beans.

Ingredients

1 lb finely ground chicken

2 oz shallots, sliced

Cilantro leaves, chopped

4 tbsp sticky rice, dry-fried for 8–10 minutes until brown and pounded finely

4 tbsp lemon juice, or to taste

3 tbsp fish sauce, or to taste

1 tbsp chopped dried red chile, or to taste

½ tsp sugar

Fresh mint leaves

Raw cabbage leaves, scallions, and raw string beans, to serve

Serves 6

Wild boar country curry

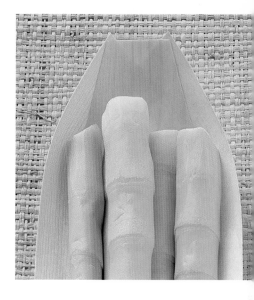

W ild boar is not strictly necessary (and in any case, tends to be bred rather than hunted in Thailand these days). You can replace it with pork or venison.

Heat the oil in a wok or pan and fry the chile paste for 3 minutes. Add the meat and stir-fry for 2 minutes; then add the water and bamboo shoots and cook until the shoots are tender, about 3–5 minutes.

Add the eggplants, string beans, krachai or ginger, chiles, fish sauce, and lime leaf. Boil for 3 minutes more and then remove from the heat. Stir in the basil and serve.

Serve accompanied by pickled garlic, salted eggs, and sticky rice (see page 86).

Ingredients

2 oz chile paste (see page 51)

4 tbsp peanut or corn oil

8 oz boar, pork, or venison loin, cut into
　1 x ¾ x ¼-in slices

2½ pints water

7 oz bamboo shoots, diced

5 oz small white eggplants

4½ oz string beans

2 oz krachai or 1 oz fresh root ginger, peeled
　and sliced lengthwise

3 fresh red chiles, quartered

2 tbsp fish sauce

3 kaffir lime leaves, torn into small pieces

2 oz basil leaves

Serves 4

Spicy pork curry

Ingredients

8 oz ground pork

Juice of 2 limes

Peanut oil for frying

4 green chiles, seeded and roughly chopped

2 shallots, thinly sliced

2 tbsp roughly chopped cilantro leaves

2 tbsp fish sauce

3 oz unsalted, roasted peanuts, roughly chopped

Sprigs of Thai basil

Serves 4

*K*nown as larb, this is the archetypal dish of northeast Thailand, where it is usually made with raw meat. However, as this recipe uses pork, for safety's sake, it's important to make sure that the meat is thoroughly cooked. Serve with sticky rice (see page 86) and a spicy green papaya salad (see page 109).

Place the pork in a mixing bowl and squeeze over three-quarters of the lime juice. Use your hands to mix the juice with the pork. Place in the fridge to marinate for 20 minutes.

Heat the oil in a skillet. Add the pork mixture and chiles and fry until thoroughly cooked, which should take around 5–6 minutes.

Transfer the mixture to a clean mixing bowl. Add the shallots, cilantro, fish sauce, the remaining lime juice, and all but a handful of peanuts. Use a wooden spoon to mix all the ingredients together.

Garnish with the remaining peanuts and the Thai basil. Serve immediately.

Spicy noodle salad with shrimp

*K*nown as yam woonsen, this is a filling and deeply savory salad. *The fish sauce is an essential flavor-enhancing ingredient. Prepare the dish at least 30 minutes before serving so the full, sweet, hot flavor has time to mature.*

Soak the noodles in warm water for 5 minutes or according to the instructions on the package. Rinse under cold water and drain.

In a bowl, combine in the fish sauce, lemon juice and sugar, add the shrimps and marinate for 5 minutes. Meanwhile, mix together the dressing ingredients in a bowl.

Heat the sunflower oil in a skillet and stir-fry the shrimp until cooked.

Put the bell pepper, celery, carrot, scallions, and noodles in a bowl and mix together. Place a lettuce leaf on each plate and spoon in the noodle mixture. Top with the shrimp, sprinkle with the cilantro, and serve with the dressing.

Ingredients

7 oz bean thread noodles
16 large fresh shrimp, shelled and deveined
1 tsp fish sauce
2 tsp freshly-squeezed lemon juice
1 tsp soft brown sugar
1 tbsp sunflower oil
1 small red bell pepper, finely chopped
2 sticks celery, finely sliced
4 oz carrots, cut into matchsticks
2 scallions, chopped
4 iceberg lettuce leaves
Fresh cilantro

For the dressing:
2 shallots, chopped fine
1 dry red chile, crushed
3 small green chiles, chopped
4 tbsp fish sauce
4 fl. oz freshly squeezed lemon juice
4½ tbsp superfine sugar
1 tbsp sunflower oil

Serves 4

Coconut sticky rice with mango, papaya, and lime

Ingredients

7 oz sticky rice (see page 86)

6 fl. oz coconut milk

1 mango, peeled and chopped

½ papaya, peeled, seeded, and chopped

Juice of 2 limes

Serves 4

*W*ith coconut, mangoes, and papaya all competing for attention, this can be a very sweet dessert, although the lime adds a welcome note of tartness.

Put the sticky rice in a bowl and pour over cold water to cover by 2 inches. Leave the rice to soak for several hours or overnight.

Drain the rice and transfer to a steamer lined with cheesecloth, spreading the grains out.

Steam for 20–25 minutes until the rice is tender. Warm the coconut milk and mix with the rice.

Leave the rice to stand for 15 minutes before serving with the mango and papaya, squeezing the lime juice over the fruit.

Fruit salad with lime and papaya sauce

Seductively aromatic when ripe, papayas are highly prized in northeastern Thai cooking, not just for their flavor but also their healing properties. An open wound is said to heal more quickly after the application of a papaya poultice.

Prepare the fruit as necessary and cut into bite-sized pieces.

To make the sauce, roughly chop the papaya flesh and place in a food processor with three-quarters of the lime zest and all the juice. Add the tropical fruit juice and reduce to a smooth purée, adjusting the amount of juice, if necessary, according to the size of the papaya.

Serve the sauce with the fruit salad and the remaining lime zest scattered over. Decorate each serving with a lime leaf.

Ingredients

For the fruit salad:
1½ lb tropical fruits, such as mango, pineapple, rambutan, longan

For the sauce:
1 ripe medium-sized papaya, peeled and seeded
Zest and juice of 2 limes, grated fine
6 fl. oz tropical fruit juice
Kaffir lime leaves, to garnish

Serves 4

CHAPTER FOUR

Central Thailand

The map on the right shows the provinces of Central Thailand with the following labels:

Chai Nat Province
Lop Buri Province
Sing Bori Province
Ang Thong Province
Nakhon Nayok Province
Kanchanaburi Province
Supban Buri Province
Saraburi Province
Prachin Buri Province
Sa Kaeo Province
Chachoengsao Province
Samut Songkhram Province
Ratchaburi Province
Chon Buri Province
Rayong Province
Chantaburi Province
Phetchaburi Province
Prachuap Khiri Khan Province
Samut Prakan Province
Bangkok Metropolis Province
Pathum Thani Province
Phra Nakhon Si Ayutthaya Province
Nonthaburi Province
Samut Sakhon Province
Nakhom Pathom Province
Trat Province

The Thai heartland, comprising the capital city Bangkok, the central plains, and the Gulf of Thailand, is the country's most visited region. As such, it has long acted as a magnet for other cultures and cuisines. The influence of China is felt particularly strongly, as shown by the great number of noodle dishes eaten here. With fresh produce in abundance—be it fish and seafood from local waters, or fruit, vegetables, and high-quality rice grown on the central plain—the region has something for all tastes and budgets. Its cuisine runs the gamut from elaborate platters of carved fruit and vegetables, as once served at the Royal Grand Palace, to simple but delicious street food sold from stalls to busy Bangkok office workers.

LEFT: Fresh fruit and vegetables are bartered at a floating Bangkok market—traditionally the only way to trade in Thailand.

Fragrant rice

*I*n the central and southern regions of Thailand, steamed, fragrant rice is preferred to the sticky rice more commonly eaten in the northern and northeastern parts of the country. If you want to cook a different quantity of rice, just remember that there should always be double the amount of water to that of rice.

Ingredients
8 oz long grain rice
1 pint cold water
Thai basil to garnish

Serves 4

Rinse the rice in a sieve until the water runs clear, then place it in a pan with the water. Bring to boil, lower the heat, and cook uncovered until the water has been absorbed and a series of holes appear in the surface of the rice.

Line the base of a steamer to within ½ inch of the edges with tin foil and raise the edges into a shallow, bowl-like shape. Puncture all over the base with a skewer. Turn the rice into the foil in the steamer and place over a pan of fairly fast bubbling water. Cover and cook for 30 minutes until the rice is just tender and fluffy. Refill the base pan with more boiling water as necessary.

Note that no salt is added to this recipe—this is the traditional method of cooking, as Thai rice is of such excellent quality, with a fragrant flavor, that salt is unnecessary.

Hot and sour noodle soup with shrimp

Ingredients

1 tbsp vegetable oil

2 cloves garlic, shredded

2 shallots, shredded

½ in fresh root ginger, thinly sliced

4–5 small red chiles, chopped

2 pints light chicken stock

3 kaffir lime leaves, sliced

4-in piece of lemongrass, chopped

7 oz rice vermicelli

20 large cooked shrimp, shell and head on

6 tbsp fish sauce

6 tbsp fresh lemon or lime juice

2 tbsp raw sugar

16 canned straw mushrooms

Fresh cilantro and kaffir lime leaves

Serves 4

The hot and sour soup known as tom yum is one of Thailand's most popular and versatile dishes. This version, made with shrimp, is known as tom yum goong, but there are plenty of others, including tom yum gai (with chicken), tom yum pla (with fish), and tum yum hed (with mushrooms). The broth on which they are all based is a myriad of textures and flavors, combining sour lime leaves, sharp lemongrass, spicy ginger, and fiery chiles.

Heat the oil in a pan. When hot, stir-fry the garlic, shallots, ginger, and chiles for 1 minute. Pour in the stock, then add the lime leaves and lemongrass. Bring to a boil and simmer for 5 minutes.

Meanwhile, soak the noodles for 3 minutes in warm water, then drain and rinse under cold water. Drain before dividing the noodles among four bowls.

Add the shrimp, fish sauce, lemon juice, sugar, and mushrooms to the stock and simmer for 2–3 minutes. Pour immediately over the noodles and sprinkle with cilantro leaves and lime leaves.

Pork and noodle soup

*T*his Thai soup, known as kwitiaow nam, is served from floating kitchens working up and down rivers and canals. This version contains three varieties of pork, but lean cuts of pork contain only the same amount of fat as chicken. Preserved cabbage and fish balls can be bought at specialty Asian food stores.

Boil the pork loin in water for about 15 minutes. Allow it to cool before cutting into ½-in wide strips. Cover and set aside.

In a pan, boil enough water to cover the noodles and bean sprouts. Add the noodles and bean sprouts and boil for 3 minutes. Drain and divide among 4 deep bowls. Top with the pork loin, pork liver, and preserved cabbage, if using.

Bring the stock to a boil. Add the fish balls and boil for 3 minutes. Remove with a slotted spoon and add to the bowls. Reserve the stock.

Put the ground pork in a pan with ¾ pint of chicken stock. Heat gently and stir until the pork is cooked, which should take around 4–5 minutes. Stir in the scallions, cilantro, garlic, and pepper to heat through. Ladle the pork mixture and stock into the bowls. Top with the remaining heated chicken stock to fill each bowl. Serve immediately.

Ingredients

7 oz lean pork loin, thinly sliced
11 oz dried rice-stick noodles
12 oz bean sprouts
4 oz pork liver, boiled and thinly sliced
1 tsp chopped preserved cabbage (optional)
4 pints chicken stock
12 fish balls
4 oz ground lean pork
1 scallion, chopped
2 tbsp coarsely chopped fresh cilantro
   leaves and stems
2 tbsp chopped garlic, fried in oil until
   golden
½ tsp ground white pepper

Serves 4

Stuffed baby squid in a broth

Squid is a popular delicacy in Thailand where it is served as an appetizer (usually barbecued dried squid), broiled as a main course, or, as in this instance, in a hot and sour broth.

Prepare the squid by removing the heads, rubbing the purplish skin, and pulling out the quill. Turn inside out and wash well. Turn back to the original side and drain well. Cut the tentacles from the head and squeeze out the center bone. Wash and reserve tentacles.

Mix the pork, finely chopped cilantro, garlic, and seasoning together. Stuff the squid with this mixture, but do not overfill. Replace the tentacles at the opening of the squid. Secure with toothpicks.

Bring the fish stock to a boil with the lemongrass. Cook for a few minutes. Drop in the squid with torn lime leaves and cook gently for 10–15 minutes. Remove the lemongrass and lime leaves, taste for seasoning, and add fish sauce or lime juice.

Serve in bowls topped with with chile rings and the reserved cilantro leaves.

Ingredients

1 lb baby squid, cleaned but left whole for
  stuffing
½ lb raw pork meat, finely ground
4 stems cilantro, leaves reserved for garnish
1–2 cloves garlic, peeled and crushed
Salt and freshly ground black pepper
2½ pints fish stock
2 stems of lemongrass, bruised
2 or 3 lime leaves
2 tbsp fish sauce or lime juice
1–2 chiles, seeded and cut into rings

Serves 6–8

Scallops with lemongrass broth and spinach

Scallops have very delicate flesh that quickly overcooks and becomes tough. Make sure the skillet is really hot, and sear the scallops quickly on each side so they are lightly golden on the outside but soft and succulent on the inside.

Put the stock, lemongrass, scallions, red chile, green bell pepper, enoki mushrooms, sugar, fish sauce, and lime juice in a saucepan and simmer for 5 minutes.

Meanwhile, heat the peanut oil in a heavy skillet and when very hot, sear the scallops for about 1 minute on each side until just cooked.

Add the spinach to the broth and continue to simmer until the leaves have just wilted. Divide between the serving dishes with the scallops served on top.

Ingredients

10 fl. oz chicken stock
1 tbsp lemongrass, finely sliced
4 scallions, chopped
Red chile, seeded and very finely chopped
½ green bell pepper, seeded and finely chopped
4 oz enoki mushrooms
½ tsp superfine sugar
1 tbsp fish sauce
Juice of 1 lime
2 tbsp peanut oil
12 scallops without roes
3 oz baby spinach leaves, washed

Serves 4

Crab cakes with chile vinegar

Ingredients

12 oz crab meat
2 tsp red curry paste (see page 156)
1 tsp grated fresh root ginger
2 tbsp chopped fresh cilantro leaves
½ tsp fish sauce
1 egg
2 tbsp plain flour
Sunflower oil, for frying

For the chile vinegar:
1 tbsp sugar
4 fl. oz rice wine vinegar
2 tsp fish sauce
2 fresh red chiles, seeded and sliced

Makes 16

*T*hese spicy little fish cakes are the perfect start to a Thai meal, but they also make a great snack to serve with cocktails.

First prepare the chile vinegar. Put the sugar, vinegar, and fish sauce in a pan and warm gently, stirring, until the sugar has dissolved. Pour into a small bowl, add the chiles, and set aside to cool.

Put the crab meat, curry paste, ginger, cilantro, and fish sauce in a bowl and mix together well using a fork. Stir in the egg, then sprinkle over the flour and mix well to combine. Shape the mixture into 16 small fish cakes.

Heat about 1 tablespoon of oil in a non-stick pan. Fry the fish cakes in batches if necessary for 2–3 minutes on each side, until golden. Drain well on paper towel and serve hot, with chile vinegar for dipping.

There are a number of variations you can try with this dish, such as adding green curry paste (see page 150) instead of red curry paste or adding chopped lemongrass or grated lime rind to the crab cake mixture. You might also like to serve it with sweet chile sauce (see page 181) in place of chile vinegar.

Fried mussel pancakes

*M*ussel and pancakes may seem an unlikely combination, but it works well using a batter made from tapioca flour. This is market food—if you stroll through the night market of any central Thailand town you can hear, and smell, the sizzling of this dish.

Mix all the batter ingredients together thoroughly (alternatively, you can use store-bought tempura batter). Heat a large, heavy skillet, preferably cast iron, and add about ½ inch of oil.

Mix 2 oz of the mussel meat and 2 fl. oz of the batter together and pour into the pan. Cook over a medium heat for about 5 minutes until brown on the bottom, then break one egg on top of the mussel cake. Flip over carefully and fry until the egg is lightly browned, which should take around 3–5 minutes. Remove the mussel cake from the pan and drain well on a paper towel. Repeat with the rest of the mussels and batter to make eight cakes.

Add the bean sprouts to the pan and fry lightly. Place on a serving plate, and arrange the mussel cakes on top. Sprinkle with the scallions and white pepper before serving.

Serve accompanied by thick chile sauce.

Ingredients
8 fl. oz peanut or corn oil for frying
1 lb raw mussel or oyster meat
8 eggs
11 oz large bean sprouts
3 tbsp scallions, finely sliced
2 tsp ground white pepper

For the batter:
1 pint water
4 oz all-purpose flour
8 oz tapioca flour or cornstarch
2 tbsp baking powder
2 tbsp sugar
2 eggs, beaten
2 tsp salt

Makes 8

Stuffed crab shells

*T*his dish is as well known in Thailand for its name, poo jag, as for anything else—it means, literally, "dear crab," for reasons that no one has ever been able to explain convincingly.

Mix all the stuffing ingredients together and fill the crab shells. Heat the oil in a pan or wok to approximately 350°F.

Dip the stuffed crabs in the beaten egg to coat them well all over, and then deep-fry until thoroughly cooked, for about 10–15 minutes. Remove and drain well on paper towel.

Sprinkle with the cilantro and chile before serving. Serve as an hors d'oeuvre or with steamed rice (see page 128) and bottled Asian plum sauce.

Ingredients
4 blue crab shells, well cleaned
3 eggs, beaten
2 pints peanut or corn oil for deep-frying
2 oz cilantro leaves
2 fresh red chiles, cut into lengthwise strips

For the stuffing:
8 oz cooked ground pork
4 oz ground shrimp
3 oz crabmeat, fresh, or drained very well if
   canned
2 tbsp onion, finely chopped
1 tbsp scallion, finely sliced
1 tsp ground white pepper
1 tsp sugar
¼ tsp light soy sauce
¼ tsp salt

Serves 4

Crab and snow pea salad

*U*se fresh white crabmeat to make the salad but pick it over carefully first in case any small sharp pieces of shell are hidden in the larger flakes of flesh.

Heat the peanut oil in a wok and stir-fry the snow peas, baby corn, and red bell pepper over a medium heat for 3 minutes.

Add the beansprouts and stir-fry for a further minute, then set aside to cool.

Break up the crabmeat into large flakes. Divide the Chinese leaves between serving plates, and top with the stir-fried vegetables and then the crab.

To make the dressing, whisk all the ingredients together until the sugar has dissolved. Pour the dressing over the salad and serve.

Ingredients

2 tbsp peanut oil

6 oz snow peas, thinly sliced lengthwise

6 oz baby corn, halved lengthwise

½ red bell pepper, seeded and thinly sliced

4 oz beansprouts

1 lb white crabmeat

½ head of Chinese leaves (also known as napa cabbage), shredded

For the dressing:

1 red chile, seeded and very finely chopped

½ tsp fresh ginger purée

8 tbsp sunflower oil

4 tbsp rice vinegar

2 tbsp light soy sauce

1 tsp superfine sugar

Serves 4

Chicken and pomelo salad with fresh cilantro, lime, and green chile dressing

Ingredients

For the dressing:

1 clove garlic, peeled and sliced

2 fresh coriander root (if available, if not use cilantro leaves), washed and dried

½ green chile, seeded

5 fl. oz fresh lime juice

2 tsp soft light brown sugar

2 tsp fish sauce

For the salad:

1 pomelo (or use 2 grapefruit)

6 oz cooked, peeled shrimp

12 oz cooked chicken, shredded

3 tbsp grated fresh coconut

Fresh cilantro leaves to garnish

Serves 4

*K*nown as yam som-o, this simple chicken salad contains pomelo, a large yellow-green citrus fruit similar to a grapefruit but with a crunchier, flakier flesh. It is served with an all-purpose salad dressing called nam jim. The proportion of ingredients in this dressing will vary according to the locality and the cook's own taste, but it is important to make sure that the dressing is neither too salty nor too sweet and that the garlic is not too dominant—adjust the balance of the ingredients as required. Instead of chicken, you could use cubes of cooked white fish or baby squid mixed with the shrimp.

To make the dressing, coarsely blend the garlic and fresh cilantro in a spice mill or pound in a mortar and pestle. Add the chiles and blend or pound again, then work in the lime juice. Add the sugar and fish sauce, and stir until the sugar dissolves.

Peel the pomelo, divide into segments and remove the papery skin. Break up the flesh into chunks. Place in a bowl, add the dressing and stir to mix. Add the shrimp, chicken and grated cocount and toss together lightly.

Spoon into a serving dish and garnish with fresh cilantro leaves.

Rice, mango, and shrimp salad with lemongrass dressing

*T*his recipe is a useful way to use up leftover cooked rice. Ensure the rice you use is less than one day old. The ingredients for the salad, which is known as khao yam paak tai, are arranged on serving plates around a mound of rice in the center so that diners can take a little of each ingredient and mix it with the rice as they wish. Dried shrimp are available from Thai food stores.

To make the dressing, place the water in a saucepan and add the fish sauce, shrimp paste, sugar, lemongrass purée, lime rind, and juice and bring to a boil. Simmer for 2 minutes, then remove from the heat and add the basil.

Place the dried shrimp in a bowl, cover with boiling water, and allow to soak for 10 minutes, then drain. Make a thin omelet out of the eggs by beating the eggs together and heating them slowly on a pan. When it has a thick consistency, remove from the pan, roll up, and slice thinly.

Divide the rice into four cups or small basins, press down to shape the rice, and turn the mounds out into the center of four large serving plates.

Arrange the soaked dried shrimp, sliced omelet, mango, bean sprouts, beans, coconut, shrimp, and pineapple in separate mounds around the rice and spoon the dressing over them. Garnish with lime wedges, fresh cilantro sprigs, and chopped red chiles.

To serve, give each diner a small plate so they can take a little rice and mix it with a selection of individual ingredients. Serve the dressing separately if preferred.

Ingredients

For the dressing:
5 fl oz water
1 tbsp fish sauce
½ tsp shrimp paste (kapi)
1 tbsp soft brown sugar
1 tsp fresh lemongrass purée
Finely grated rind and juice of 1 lime
1 tbsp finely torn Thai basil

For the salad:
3 tbsp dried shrimp
2 large eggs
1 lb cooked rice, chilled
1 under-ripe (green) mango, peeled and the flesh sliced away from the pit
4 oz bean sprouts
4 oz cooked green beans, sliced
4 tbsp shaved fresh coconut flesh, lightly toasted
4 oz cooked, peeled shrimp
1 slice pineapple, cut into small pieces
Lime wedges, fresh cilantro sprigs, and chopped red chiles to garnish

Serves 4

Tofu salad in garlic, chile, and lime dressing

Ingredients
100 g (4 oz) baby corn, cut into halves
10 oz firm tofu, cut into ½-in cubes
2 oz shredded iceberg lettuce
1 carrot, peeled and shredded
½ green bell pepper, thinly sliced
6 cherry tomatoes, halved
1 shallot, thinly sliced
3 tbsp cilantro leaves
2 tbsp roasted peanuts, roughly chopped, to
   garnish

For the dressing:
1 clove garlic, finely chopped
½ fresh small red chile
1 stalk lemongrass, finely chopped
1 tbsp freshly squeezed lime juice
2 tsp soft brown sugar
1 tbsp fish sauce
2 tbsp sunflower oil

Serves 4

*T*he tofu and spicy dressing greatly enhance the taste and texture of this otherwise rather basic salad dish.

Boil the baby corn in a pan of boiling water for 4–5 minutes, then drain. Blanch the tofu in another pan of boiling water and drain this.

In a bowl, mix the lettuce, carrot, bell pepper, tomatoes, shallot, cilantro, baby corn, and tofu.

Place the garlic, chile, lemongrass, lime juice, sugar, fish sauce, and oil in a bowl, and mix well. Pour the dressing over the salad and sprinkle with the peanuts just before serving.

LEFT: A street vendor in Bangkok mixes together a garlic, chile, and lime dressing for a fresh mango salad.

Spicy mussel salad

*Q*uick to prepare and delightfully fresh-tasting, this spicy mussel salad, known as yam hoi mang pu, is usually served in Thailand as an appetizer rather than as part of a main meal.

Steam the mussels in their shells in batches, placing a single layer of mussels in the bottom of the pan each time. Do not pile the mussels up. Steam for around 5 minutes or until all (or most) of the shells have opened. Drain and remove the meat from the opened shells. Discard any unopened shells.

Mix together the rest of the salad ingredients, except for the cabbage, in a bowl. Taste for seasoning, adding extra lime juice or fish sauce if required. Add the mussels and serve on a platter, with the cabbage leaves around the edge to be eaten with the salad.

Ingredients

15 oz cooked mussel meat (from approx 3½ lb
   mussels in their shells)
10 fresh small green chiles, finely chopped
1 oz mint leaves
3 tbsp lime or lemon juice, or to taste
2½ tbsp fish sauce, or to taste
2 tbsp shallots, sliced
2 tbsp ginger, cut into matchsticks
2 tbsp lemongrass, finely sliced
½ tbsp kaffir lime leaves, shredded
1 small head of white Chinese (also known as
   napa) cabbage, cut into wedges
½ small head of green cabbage, cut into
   wedges

Serves 4

Scallops with Thai basil, cilantro, and garlic

*T*hai basil has deep-green, oval-shaped leaves with purple stems running through them. It has a much stronger flavor than the Mediterranean variety, with a strong perfume of aniseed. If you struggle to find Thai basil, substitute garlic chives. Mediterranean sweet basil could be used, but it will give the dish a different flavor.

Mix together the fish sauce, dark soy sauce, and sugar until the sugar dissolves.

Heat half the peanut oil in a skillet and fry the shallots and yellow bell pepper over a medium heat for 3 minutes. Add the garlic and red chile and fry for a further 2–3 minutes until the vegetables are just tender. Remove from the skillet and set aside.

Increase the heat under the skillet, add the remaining oil, and when very hot, sear the scallops on each side until lightly browned.

Pour the fish sauce mixture over the scallops and stir until they are coated. Return the vegetables to the skillet, add the basil and cilantro, and cook for 1 minute.

Serve hot with steamed rice and a salad.

Ingredients

2 tbsp fish sauce

2 tbsp dark soy sauce

½ tsp sugar

2 tbsp peanut oil

4 red shallots, peeled and sliced

½ yellow bell pepper, seeded and finely chopped

2 garlic cloves, peeled and chopped

1 red chile, seeded and chopped fine

16–20 small (queen) scallops

2 tbsp coarsely chopped Thai basil

2 tbsp coarsely chopped cilantro leaves

Serves 2

Green curry paste

*T*hai cuisine has a reputation for being fiery and the country's curry dishes are no exception. Chiles are the culprit so the "heat" of the finished dish will depend on the type of chiles used and whether you add their seeds or discard them. As a rule of thumb, the smaller the chile, the hotter it is. Curries in Thailand are color coded into green, red, and yellow varieties—the difference being the color of the chiles used to make the basic curry paste. Green curries are made from fresh green chiles ground with fresh cilantro, red curries from red chiles, and yellow from fresh yellow chiles (or sometimes red) given a boost with ground turmeric. When the word "gaeng" is included in the curry's title it means the sauce is based on a creamy coconut broth.

Ingredients

6 medium green chiles, seeded and coarsely
  chopped
2 stalks lemongrass, outer leaves removed,
  and chopped
Small bunch fresh cilantro, stalks removed
Small bunch Thai basil, stalks removed
1 shallot, peeled and chopped
1 tsp coriander seeds
1 tsp cumin seeds
2 large cloves garlic, peeled and
  coarsely chopped
1 tsp shrimp paste (kapi)
1-in piece fresh galangal, peeled and chopped
  or 2 tsp galangal purée
4 kaffir lime leaves, chopped

Makes 4 fl. oz

Put all the ingredients in a food processor and blend to a paste. Alternatively, pound the ingredients using a mortar and pestle.

Store the paste in a sealed container in the refrigerator and use as needed. It will keep for up to 3 weeks.

Green beef curry

*D*efinitely green, this is one of the basic Thai curry styles, and can be used equally well to make a curry with pork, chicken, or duck instead of beef.

Heat ½ pint of the coconut milk in a pan, add the chile paste, and cook for 2 minutes. Add the beef and the rest of the coconut milk, and bring to a boil.

Add the fish sauce and jaggery, boil for 2 more minutes, then add the eggplant and chile, and cook for 1 minute. Stir in the lime leaf, boil for 1 minute, add the basil and remove from the heat.

Serve in bowls accompanied by steamed rice, pickled vegetables, salted eggs, and sun-dried beef.

Ingredients
2 pints thin coconut milk
Green chile paste (see opposite)
11 oz beef sirloin, cut into 1 x ¾ x ¼ in slices
2 tbsp fish sauce
½ tbsp jaggery (or soft brown sugar)
10 small white eggplants, quartered
3 fresh red chiles, quartered lengthwise
3 kaffir lime leaves, torn into small pieces
2 tbsp sweet basil leaves

Serves 4

Green curry with shrimp, pumpkin, and zucchini

Not all green curries are the same—there's plenty of room for variation around the basic theme. This shrimp-based recipe uses pumpkin and zucchini to give added texture. The Thai basil garnish provides a pleasant, aniseed-like aroma.

Heat the peanut oil in a large skillet, add the shallot and pumpkin or butternut squash, and fry for 5 minutes, stirring occasionally.

Add the zucchini and green curry paste and fry for a further 2 minutes, stirring to make sure the paste does not stick.

Stir in the fish sauce, sugar, and coconut milk. Bring to a boil, lower the heat, and simmer for 15 minutes until the pumpkin or butternut squash is tender.

Add the shrimp and simmer for 2–3 minutes until they turn pink. Serve garnished with the scallions, green chile, and Thai basil leaves.

Ingredients

2 tbsp peanut oil

3 red shallots, peeled and sliced

7 oz pumpkin or butternut squash, peeled, seeded, and cut into small pieces

1 zucchini, sliced

2 tbsp green chile paste (see page 150)

1 tbsp fish sauce

1 tbsp soft brown sugar

14 fl. oz coconut milk

1 lb raw peeled shrimp

2 scallions, shredded

1 green chile, seeded and finely sliced

Thai basil leaves

Serves 4

Green curry with chicken

Ingredients

2 tbsp peanut oil

2 shallots, peeled and sliced

1 sweet potato, peeled and cut into small
pieces

1 zucchini, trimmed and sliced

2 tbsp green curry paste (see page 150)

1 lb 2 oz boneless chicken thighs, skinned and
cut into chunks

1 tbsp fish sauce

2 tbsp jaggery or soft brown sugar

14 fl. oz coconut milk

3 kaffir lime leaves, shredded

1 red chile, seeded and finely sliced

Serves 6

This is the most famous and most widely eaten of all the green curry recipes, known in Thailand as gaeng kheow wan gai. Despite its fame, it still allows for a good deal of flexibility. A selection of firm white fish or shellfish can easily be substituted for the chicken without needing to change the basic recipe—simply make sure that you add the fish or shellfish around 5 minutes before the curry is cooked, so that it will not overcook and become tough and tasteless. Also, avoid stirring the curry too frequently once the white fish has been added or its delicate flesh will break and disintegrate.

Heat the oil in a large saucepan, add the shallots and sweet potato, and fry over a gentle heat for 5 minutes, stirring occasionally. Add the zucchini and curry paste and fry for a further 2 minutes.

Add the chicken, stirring so it is evenly coated in the spice paste, and fry for 5 minutes.

Stir in the fish sauce, sugar, and coconut milk and bring to a boil.

Lower the heat and simmer gently for 15 minutes until the chicken and sweet potato are done and the sauce has reduced and thickened a little.

Serve at once garnished with the shredded lime leaves and chile.

Fried vermicelli
with red curry paste

*T*hough it may look more fiery, there is no reason why red curry
paste should be any hotter than the green version. Its precise
heat level is entirely down to your own personal taste—remember
more chiles equals more heat. If you really feel like testing your
tastebuds, try adding the chile seeds as well.

To make the curry paste, put all the ingredients in a food processor and blend to a paste. Alternatively, pound the ingredients using a mortar and pestle.

Soak the rice vermicelli in warm water for 3–5 minutes. Rinse, and drain.

Heat the oil in a wok or skillet, and fry the tofu until golden brown. Add the garlic, bamboo shoots, bean sprouts, and mustard greens or spinach, stirring each time you add the ingredients.

Add the red curry paste, fish sauce, soy sauce, and sugar and stir well. Add the vermicelli and stir until the noodles are well coated with the sauce. Put the vermicelli onto four plates and garnish with cilantro leaves and lime wedges. Serve at once.

Ingredients

For the paste:

4–6 medium red chiles, seeded (optional) and coarsely chopped

2 oz shallots, coarsely chopped

1 tbsp coriander root (or fresh leaves)

2 kaffir lime leaves

2 stalks lemongrass, outer leaves removed, coarsely chopped

1 tsp coriander seeds

1 tsp cumin seeds

2 large cloves garlic, coarsely chopped

1 tbsp shrimp paste (kapi)

1 tbsp galangal purée or 1-in piece of fresh root ginger, coarsely chopped

2 cloves garlic, peeled and chopped

¼ tsp salt

For the noodles:

8 oz rice vermicelli

3 tbsp vegetable oil

8 oz tofu (bean curd), diced

3 cloves garlic, chopped

4 oz canned bamboo shoots

1½ lb bean sprouts

8 oz mustard greens or fresh spinach

2 tbsp red curry paste

6 tbsp fish sauce

3 tbsp light soy sauce

1 tbsp jaggery or soft brown sugar

Cilantro leaves

4 lime wedges

Serves 4

Red curry with tofu

Ingredients
Salt
½ eggplant, chopped
1 tbsp sunflower oil
1 clove garlic, finely chopped
1 shallot, sliced
12 oz firm tofu, diced into 1-in cubes
4 oz canned bamboo shoots
2 tbsp red curry paste (see page 156)
14 fl. oz coconut milk
2 tbsp fish sauce
1 tsp soft brown sugar
1 kaffir lime leaf
1 tsp freshly squeezed lime juice
1 tbsp cilantro leaves, for garnish

Serves 4

This recipe has been influenced by both Thai and Chinese cooking. The result is a novel combination of heat and sourness.

Sprinkle the salt over the eggplant pieces and leave for 15–20 minutes before lightly rinsing. Heat the oil in a pan and fry the garlic and shallot for 1 minute.

Add the tofu, bamboo shoots, and red curry paste, and stir-fry for 1 minute.

Add the coconut milk, fish sauce, sugar, lime leaf, and lime juice. Bring to a boil and simmer for 15–20 minutes.

Garnish with cilantro and serve with steamed rice (see page 128).

Red vegetable curry with squash and sweet potato

*T*his curry can be served on its own as a vegetarian meal or as an accompaniment to a spicy meat or fish dish. Be sure to cut the squash and sweet potato into small pieces so that they cook quickly and evenly.

Heat the peanut oil in a deep skillet or large saucepan, add the red curry paste and onion and fry over a low heat for 2–3 minutes until the onion starts to soften. Add the sweet potato and butternut squash and fry for a further 10 minutes, stirring occasionally.

Add the green bell pepper, zucchini, and shiitake mushrooms, fry for 2 minutes, then add the fish sauce, lime juice, sugar, lemongrass, and coconut milk.

Cover the pan and leave the curry to simmer gently for 10–15 minutes or until the vegetables are tender. Garnish with the red onion, red chile, and coconut. Serve with steamed rice (see page 128).

Ingredients

2 tbsp peanut oil
2 tbsp red curry paste (see page 156)
1 red onion, peeled and sliced
1 sweet potato, peeled and cut into ¾-in dice
7 oz butternut squash, peeled, seeded, and cut into ¾-in dice
1 green bell pepper, seeded and chopped
1 zucchini, chopped
4 oz shiitake mushrooms, sliced
2 tbsp fish sauce
1 tbsp lime juice
2 tsp superfine sugar
1 tsp lemongrass, sliced fine
12 fl. oz coconut milk
1 tbsp red onion, finely chopped
1 red chile, seeded and finely chopped
2 tbsp shredded fresh coconut or desiccated coconut

Serves 4

Sweet and sour chicken

Ingredients

8 fl. oz peanut or corn oil

15 oz skinless, boneless chicken breasts, cut
   across into ¼-in slices

All-purpose flour for coating

1 medium-sized onion, sliced

1 medium-sized green bell pepper, sliced

3 tbsp ketchup

1 large carrot, thinly chopped

4 oz tomato quarters

4 oz pineapple, chopped

4 fl. oz chicken stock

2 tsp light soy sauce

1 tsp sugar

1 tsp vinegar

Serves 4–6

A Thai take on this popular Asian dish. It is not an overly spicy recipe, but a spoonful of fish sauce will add zest.

Heat the oil in a wok or pan, coat the chicken lightly with flour, and fry it until it is light brown, which should take around 5 minutes. Remove and drain on paper towel.

Remove all the oil except for about 4 tablespoons. Add the onion and bell pepper, cook for 1 minute. Mix in the ketchup, and then add the remaining ingredients. Stir-fry for 1 minute, add the chicken, and continue to cook until the onion is tender, which should take about 2 minutes.

Serve accompanied by rice and fish sauce with fresh chiles (see page 28).

Fried rice-stick noodles with shrimp

*A*lso known as pad thai, this is the best-known of all Thai noodle dishes. The key to a tasty pad thai lies in the use of salty dried shrimp and roasted peanuts. Adjust the amount of chile used to suit your palate. It is quick and easy to prepare, and is usually eaten as a secondary rather than as a main dish.

Mix together the marinade ingredients, and marinate the shrimp for at least 15 minutes.

Soak the noodles in warm water for 2–5 minutes, or according to the instructions on the package. Rinse under cold water and drain.

Heat 2 tablespoons of the oil in a wok or skillet, and stir-fry the garlic and shallots for 30 seconds. Make a well in the middle and pour in the eggs. Lightly scramble without incorporating the garlic and shallots. Stir in the peanuts, chiles, dried shrimp, scallions, and bean sprouts.

Add 1 tablespoon of oil to the wok, and stir in the noodles. Add the sugar, fish sauce, and lemon juice, and stir to coat the noodles. Push to one side while the marinated shrimp are stir-fried in the remaining tablespoon of oil.

Divide the noodles among four plates and top with the shrimp, cilantro leaves, and lime wedges. Serve immediately.

Ingredients
For the marinade:
1 tsp freshly squeezed lemon juice
1 tsp fish sauce
½ tsp soft brown sugar

12 large cooked shrimp, shelled and
   deveined, tails intact
10 oz dried, rice-stick noodles
4 tbsp vegetable oil
3 cloves garlic, crushed
4 shallots, sliced
2 eggs, beaten
2 tbsp roasted peanuts, crushed
3–4 small green chiles, chopped
2 tbsp dried shrimp, chopped
2 scallions, chopped
7 oz bean sprouts
2½ tbsp soft brown sugar
6 tbsp fish sauce
4 fl. oz freshly squeezed lemon juice
Fresh cilantro leaves
4 lime wedges

Serves 2

Casseroled shrimp with bean-thread noodles

*T*his recipe, known as kung op woon sen in Thailand, makes four generous servings. The size of the shrimp is unimportant, and lobster tails or crab claws can be substituted. But for maximum flavor, use fresh, not frozen, produce.

Place the soup stock ingredients in a pan and bring to a boil. Simmer for 5 minutes, then set aside to cool.

In a heat-proof casserole dish or heavy saucepan, lay out the bacon so that it covers the base. Top with the shrimp, coriander root, ginger, garlic, and peppercorns. Cover with noodles, then add the butter, soy sauce, and soup stock.

Place on the heat, cover, and bring to a boil. Simmer for 5 minutes, then mix well, and sprinkle with chopped cilantro. Cover and cook for 5 minutes, or until the shrimp are cooked through. Remove any excess soup stock before serving.

Ingredients

For the soup stock:
1 pint chicken stock
2 tbsp oyster sauce
1½ tbsp dark soy sauce
½ tbsp sesame oil
½ tsp sugar

For the shrimp and noodles:
2 bacon strips, cut into 1-in pieces
20 large fresh shrimp, shelled
    and deveined
2 fresh coriander roots, rinsed and halved
1 oz fresh root ginger, finely chopped
1 clove garlic, chopped
1 tsp white peppercorns, crushed
8 oz bean-thread noodles (also known as
    cellophane or glass noodles), soaked
    in hot water for 5 minutes
1 tsp butter
2 tbsp dark soy sauce
2 tbsp fresh cilantro, roughly chopped

Serves 4

Sweet crisp-fried vermicelli with shrimp and cashew nuts

*A*lthough it requires a little more time than most noodle dishes, this rice vermicelli dish is well worth the extra effort. It is essential that it is served as soon as it is ready as the vermicelli will become mushy if left for very long.

Heat the vegetable oil in a wok or saucepan until very hot. Deep-fry the vermicelli for a few seconds until they puff up and become white. Drain on paper towel.

Heat the tablespoon of oil in a wok or skillet. Add the garlic and shallots, and stir. Add the shrimp and cashew nuts, and stir-fry for about 2 minutes.

Add the sugar, lemon juice, vinegar, soy sauce, ketchup, and chili powder, and simmer until the sauce thickens. Take out the shrimp, and set aside.

Add the crispy vermicelli, and coat with the sauce. Put the vermicelli on a bed of lettuce on four plates. Garnish each serving with three shrimp, cilantro, and tomato wedges.

Ingredients

For the sauce:
3 tbsp jaggery or soft brown sugar
2 tbsp freshly squeezed lemon juice
1 tsp vinegar
1 tsp light soy sauce
2 tbsp tomato ketchup
½ tsp chili powder

For the noodles:
Vegetable oil for deep-frying
2 oz rice vermicelli, slightly crushed
1 tbsp vegetable oil
2 cloves garlic, finely chopped
2 shallots, finely chopped
12 tiger or jumbo shrimp with tails, peeled and deveined
4 tbsp raw cashew nuts
2 lettuce leaves, halved
Cilantro
2 small tomato wedges

Serves 4

Sweet crisp-fried vermicelli with shrimp, pork, and tofu

This is a Thai embellishment of a Chinese dish, and for complete success depends on the noodles being fried just right—so that they are both crisp and puffy when served.

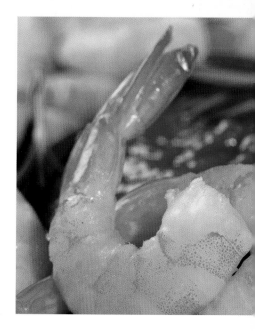

Heat the oil in a pan or wok and fry the shrimp and pork until brown and well cooked, which should take about 10 minutes.

Remove with a slotted spoon and drain on paper towel. Set aside.

Add the tofu to the hot oil and fry until brown, which should take around 2 minutes. Remove with a slotted spoon and drain on paper towel.

Add the noodles to the hot oil and brown lightly for around 4–5 minutes. Remove and drain well on paper towel.

Remove all the oil from the pan except for 2 tablespoons. Add the garlic and onion and fry gently for 1 minute; then add pork, shrimp, tofu, jaggery, vinegar, marinated soybeans, and fish sauce. Fry until thick and sticky, which should take around 7–10 minutes.

Reduce the heat and add the noodles. Mix well for 1 minute, then transfer on to a large plate in a mound. Arrange the bean sprouts, scallions, pickled garlic, and chiles on top.

Ingredients

Peanut or corn oil for deep-frying
7 oz raw medium-sized shrimp, shelled and cut into 3 pieces
5 oz pork loin, cut into cubes the same size as the shrimp pieces
4 oz firm tofu (bean curd), cut into small rectangles
5 oz thin rice vermicelli noodles, if dried soak first in cool water for 1 minute
½ tbsp garlic, chopped
½ tbsp onion, chopped
2 oz jaggery (or soft brown sugar)
2 tbsp white vinegar
1 tbsp marinated soybeans
1 tbsp fish sauce
1½ lb bean sprouts
3 scallions, cut into 1½-in pieces
2 tbsp pickled garlic, sliced
2 fresh red chiles, cut into very thin strips.

Serves 4–6

Grilled swordfish with lime and cilantro

Ingredients

4 6-oz swordfish steaks
1 tbsp peanut oil
1 tbsp fish sauce
2 tbsp dark soy sauce
2 tsp soft brown sugar
2 tbsp freshly squeezed lime juice
2 tbsp chopped fresh cilantro
1 red chile, seeded and very finely sliced
3 oz fresh spinach leaves
Lemon or lime wedges, to garnish

Serves 2

*F*ish and citrus fruits make natural partners, and fresh lime goes particularly well with an oily, firm-fleshed fish like swordfish. *Serve accompanied with spinach.*

Place the swordfish steaks side by side in a shallow dish. Mix the peanut oil, fish sauce, dark soy sauce, brown sugar, lime juice, cilantro leaves, and red chile together, and pour over the fish. Cover and leave to marinate in a cool place for 1–2 hours.

Lift the fish from the marinade, place on a grill rack or in a hot ridged grill pan and cook for 2–3 minutes on each side, depending on the thickness of the steaks, until just cooked through.

Meanwhile, pour the marinade left in the dish into a wok and boil until reduced by half. Add the spinach leaves and simmer until wilted.

Spoon the spinach onto serving plates, place the swordfish steaks on top, and spoon over any juices left in the wok. Serve garnished with lemon or lime pieces.

"Jackfruit seeds"

*T*hese sweet candies are one of a range of Thai sweetmeats made
with mung beans and egg yolks. Kanoon, or jackfruit, is not
used in the recipe—they are only called after the fruit because of
their similar shapes.

Soak the mung beans in water for 1 hour, then drain and steam them for 20 minutes or
until soft. Mash or purée in a food processor.

Put the beans in a pan with 1 lb of the sugar and the coconut milk. Bring to a boil and
then simmer, stirring, until reduced to a paste. This should take about 15 minutes—be
careful not to burn the mixture. Remove from the heat and leave to cool.

Meanwhile, make the syrup. Boil the water with the remaining sugar until reduced
by half. Remove 8 fl. oz of the syrup and put to one side. Keep the remaining syrup
simmering slowly.

Take pieces of the bean paste and shape them into small fingertip-sized ovals. Cook
them in batches of 8–10 at a time. Dip them first into the egg yolk and then drop them
into the pan of syrup. Wait until they float to the top, then remove with a slotted spoon
and drain on paper towel. Place them in the reserved cup of syrup for 30 minutes,
remove, set aside and allow to dry for 5 minutes.

Serve immediately or cover and refrigerate; serve at room temperature.

Ingredients
1 lb dried yellow mung beans
2½ lb sugar
2 pints thin coconut milk
2½ pints water
10 egg yolks, duck if possible, whisked lightly

Serves 6–8

CHAPTER FIVE

Southern Thailand

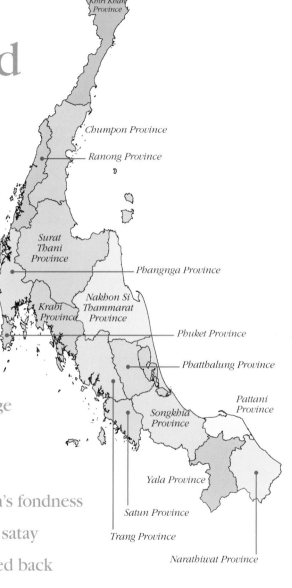

Three influences dominate the cuisine of southern Thailand: climate, coastline, and neighboring countries. Coconuts grow well in the south's tropical heat and their various elements—the milk, the flesh, and the oil—feature in many dishes. Everyday, the region's fishing boats haul ashore a great wealth of fish and seafood, more of which is eaten here than in any other part of the country. However, the large Muslim population means that little pork is consumed. The culinary heritage of surrounding countries, particularly India, is shown in the south's fondness for fiercely spiced curries, while the popularity of satay and other dishes that feature peanuts, can be traced back to Indonesia, to the region's south.

Prachuap Khiri Khan Province

Chumpon Province

Ranong Province

Surat Thani Province

Phangnga Province

Nakhon Si Thammarat Province

Krabi Province

Phuket Province

Phatthalung Province

Pattani Province

Songkhla Province

Yala Province

Satun Province

Trang Province

Narathiwat Province

LEFT: Fishing boats at dusk off a beach in Koh Samui—one of the largest islands off the coast of southern Thailand.

Coconut and galangal soup

*T**his creamy soup is a firm favorite on southern Thailand's restaurant menus, not least because of the delicate aroma and flavor provided by the galangal.*

Pour the coconut milk into a pan and bring to a boil. Add the shallots, galangal, lemongrass, chile, lime leaf, and salt.

Bring to a boil, add the chicken and then bring to a boil again. Add the mushrooms and bring it back to a boil for a final 2 minutes.

Remove from the heat and stir in the lime juice, fish sauce, and cilantro.

Serve in bowls accompanied by rice, lime quarters, and fish sauce with chiles (see page 28).

Ingredients

2½ pints thin coconut milk

1 oz shallots, finely chopped

½ oz galangal, finely sliced

2 stalks lemongrass, cut into ¾-in pieces

6 fresh small whole red chiles

3 kaffir lime leaves, torn into small pieces

1 tsp salt

11 oz skinless, boneless chicken breasts, cut across into ¼-in thick slices

7 oz fresh mushrooms (oyster if available)

2 tbsp lime or lemon juice

½ tbsp fish sauce

3 tbsp cilantro leaves and stems cut into ¾-in pieces

Serves 4–6

Chicken satay

Ingredients

1 lb skinless, boneless chicken breasts, cut into
  3 x ¾ x ¼-in long slices
12 fl. oz thin coconut milk
5 kaffir lime leaves, roughly chopped
5 cilantro roots, crushed
2 stalks of lemongrass, roughly chopped
1 tbsp curry powder
1 tsp jaggery (or soft brown sugar)
½ tsp salt

For the satay sauce:
3 oz dried yellow mung beans
2½ pints thin coconut milk
8 oz unsalted roasted peanuts,
  very finely chopped
4 oz red chile paste (see page 51)
2 oz red curry paste (see page 156)
3 tbsp jaggery (or soft brown sugar)
2 tsp tamarind juice
1 tsp salt

For the ajaad salad:
1 pint white vinegar
3 oz sugar
1 tsp salt
1 small cucumber, quartered and sliced
  lengthwise
2 oz shallots, sliced
2 fresh red chiles, thinly sliced into circles

Serves 4–6

Now popular all over Thailand, and a speciality of market food stalls, satay arrived in the south from Indonesia, via Malaysia. The dish can be made just as well with pork, tiger shrimp, tofu, or beef. Serve accompanied by a Thai ajaad salad.

Mix the chicken slices with all the other ingredients in a bowl and leave to marinate for 3–4 hours. Then carefully skewer the meat onto wood or metal skewers and broil, preferably over charcoal.

While the chicken is marinating, make the satay sauce. Soak the mung beans in water for 1 hour, then drain and steam them for 20 minutes or until soft. Purée in a food processor. Mix the mung bean purée and all the remaining satay sauce ingredients together and boil in a pan or wok for 5 minutes. Remove from the heat and leave to cool.

To make the ajaad salad, boil the vinegar, sugar, and salt together in a pan until reduced to about 8 fl. oz. Take off the heat, cool, and mix with the cucumber, shallots, and chiles.

Serve the chicken skewers with the satay sauce, ajaad salad, and pieces of toasted bread.

Sweetcorn cakes with peanut sauce

If serving the peanut sauce cold, remember it will thicken upon standing so you will need to stir in a few tablespoons of warm water to thin it down to the right consistency.

In a bowl, mix together the corn, green curry paste, fish sauce, brown sugar, cilantro, and snow peas. Stir in the flour until the ingredients are coated and then the egg to bind them together.

To make the sauce, heat the oil in a saucepan and fry the onion until softened. Add the garlic and chile and cook for 1 minute, then stir in the peanut butter, brown sugar, fish sauce, and coconut milk. Heat gently, stirring frequently so the ingredients are evenly combined.

Heat the oil for deep-frying to 350°F. Drop tablespoons of the sweetcorn mixture into the hot oil and fry for 3–4 minutes until golden brown. Drain and serve with the peanut sauce, and garnished with the chopped chile, scallions, cilantro sprigs, and extra corn kernels.

Ingredients

For the cakes:
8 snow peas, finely chopped
4 oz corn kernels with peppers
1 tbsp green curry paste (see page 150)
1 tbsp fish sauce
1 tsp soft brown sugar
1 tbsp chopped fresh cilantro
3 oz all-purpose flour
1 egg, beaten
Oil for deep-frying

For the peanut sauce:
1 small onion, finely chopped
1 garlic clove, crushed
1 small red chile, seeded and finely chopped
1 tbsp oil
4 tbsp crunchy peanut butter
2 tsp soft brown sugar
1 tsp fish sauce
4 fl. oz coconut milk

For the garnish:
Red chile, finely chopped
Scallions, shredded
Cilantro sprigs
Corn kernels

Serves 4–6

Deep-fried tempeh with sweet chile sauce

Ingredients

For the sauce:

4 fl. oz rice vinegar

4 oz sugar

3 large, pasilla chiles (see page 20), seeded

¼ cucumber, peeled, seeded, and grated

For the tempeh:

12 oz tempeh

Oil for deep-frying

2 butter lettuce leaves

1 tomato, sliced

1½ in cucumber, sliced

Serves 4

*S*weet chile sauce is the usual condiment served with snacks sold at street food stalls in Thailand. It is packaged in small plastic bags for dipping on the go, or for pouring over a more leisurely sit-down snack. Like tofu, tempeh is made from soybeans—but tempeh is a whole soybean product with a firmer texture and a stronger flavor.

To make the chile sauce, put the vinegar and sugar in a saucepan and heat gently until the sugar dissolves. Add the chiles and simmer for 10 minutes. Remove from the heat. Once cool, purée in a blender or food processor, and then stir in the grated cucumber.

Cut the tempeh in half, then slice into 1-in pieces. Heat the oil to 325°F.

Deep-fry the tempeh for about 5 minutes or until golden brown. Drain well on paper towel. Arrange the tempeh on a bed of lettuce and garnish with the sliced tomato and cucumber.

Serve the chile sauce in a small side dish.

Tempeh and vegetable salad with peanut dressing

*T*he secret of this recipe is to stop cooking the vegetables when they are still crisp rather than waiting until they get too soft.

Heat the oil in a skillet. Shallow-fry the tempeh until golden brown. Drain thoroughly on paper towel.

Cook the baby corn, carrots, zucchini, and bean sprouts in a pan of boiling water for 3–4 minutes. Add the bell pepper for the final minute. Drain well.

Mix the peanut butter, soy sauce, sugar, lemon juice, water, and chili powder together and shake well in a jar.

Place the lettuce and sliced tomatoes on a serving plate and arrange the blanched vegetables and tempeh on the top. Drizzle the peanut dressing over the salad.

Serve immediately.

Ingredients
Oil for shallow frying
12 oz tempeh, cut into bite-sized pieces
8 oz baby corn, cut into halves
8 oz carrot, peeled and shredded
1 zucchini, shredded
8 oz bean sprouts, rinsed
1 green bell pepper, seeded and sliced

For the peanut dressing:
6 tbsp peanut butter
2 tbsp light soy sauce
3 tbsp sugar
3 tbsp freshly squeezed lemon juice
4 fl. oz water
¼ tsp ground chili powder
Butter lettuce and sliced tomatoes,
    to garnish

Serves 4

RIGHT: Fishing boats in the town of Krabi, southern Thailand. With access to the Krabi River and the Andamon Sea, this is an ideal spot for fresh seafood.

Fish cakes with sweet chile dipping sauce

Ingredients

8 oz salmon fillet, skinned

8 oz firm white fish fillet, such as flounder, sole, or monkfish, skinned

1 tsp fresh ginger purée

1 tsp fresh lemongrass purée

2 kaffir lime leaves, very finely shredded

1 tbsp fish sauce

4 oz fine green beans, trimmed and finely chopped

1 tbsp chopped fresh cilantro

1 egg white, lightly beaten

Oil for shallow-frying

Lime wedges

Sweet chile sauce (see page 180)

Makes 20

*T*aud mun is the Thai name for these tiny, bite-sized fish cakes. They make an excellent snack to serve with drinks or as an appetizer. In this recipe, salmon and white fish are mixed with spices and lime leaves, but different combinations of fish can be used. You can use all white fish rather than a mix of white and salmon, or replace some of the fish with white crabmeat, prepared squid, or raw medium-sized shrimp if you prefer. The lime, however, is an important flavoring in this recipe, so if you cannot find fresh lime leaves, use the finely grated rind of two limes instead.

Cut the salmon and white fish into chunks and place in a food processor with the ginger purée, lemongrass purée, and lime leaves. Mix until coarsely ground.

Transfer to a bowl and stir in the fish sauce, green beans, fresh cilantro, and egg white.

Shape into small balls and then flatten into cakes roughly ½-in thick. Shallow fry in hot oil for 2 minutes each side until golden. Drain on paper towel and serve with lime wedges and the sweet chile dipping sauce.

Spicy fish cakes with cilantro soy dipping sauce

A mixture of salmon and a firm white fish, such as cod, is used here but you could just use salmon if you prefer. These are perhaps best served as a starter with a small salad garnish and the dipping sauce spooned over.

Cut the salmon and white fish into chunks. Trim and finely chop the green beans.

Place the salmon, white fish, lemongrass purée, ginger purée, and lime rind in a food processor and whizz until coarsely ground—be careful not to reduce the mixture to a paste. Transfer to a bowl and stir in the fish sauce, cilantro, green beans, and egg white.

With floured hands, shape into small balls and flatten into round cakes, about ½-in thick. Chill for 1 hour.

To make the dip, toast the coriander seeds in a dry, heavy-bottomed skillet until golden. Remove from the pan and mix with the soy sauce, vinegar, and sugar, stirring until the sugar dissolves. Pour into a serving bowl and float a few fresh cilantro leaves on top.

Heat oil for deep-frying to 325°F. Fry in batches for 2–3 minutes until golden. Drain and serve with the dipping sauce.

Ingredients

8 oz salmon fillet, skinned

8 oz firm white fish fillet, such as haddock or plaice

4 oz fine green beans

1 tsp fresh lemongrass purée

1 tsp fresh ginger purée

Rind of 1 lime, finely shredded

1 tbsp fish sauce

1 tbsp chopped fresh cilantro

1 egg white, lightly beaten

All-purpose flour, to dust

Oil for deep-frying

For the dipping sauce:

1 tbsp coriander seeds

4 tbsp dark soy sauce

1 tbsp white wine vinegar

½ tsp sugar

A few fresh cilantro leaves, chopped

Makes 20

Shrimp skewers with coconut rice

Ingredients

1½ oz raw tiger shrimp, peeled and deveined but tails left on
1 tsp fresh lemongrass purée
1 tsp fresh galangal purée
2 tsp green chile paste (see page 150)
1 tbsp fish sauce
1 oz creamed coconut
1½ pints vegetable stock
8 oz Thai fragrant rice (see page 128)
2 tbsp chopped fresh cilantro
1 green chile, seeded and chopped fine

Serves 4

*T*hese tangy shrimp skewers work very well served with steamed, fragrant rice and enlivened with a little bit of creamed coconut.

Thread the tiger shrimp onto skewers and place side-by-side in a shallow dish.

Mix together the lemongrass purée, galangal purée, chile paste, and fish sauce and spread over the shrimp. Cover and leave to marinate for 1 hour.

Place the creamed coconut and vegetable stock in a large saucepan and heat gently until the coconut dissolves. Rinse the Thai fragrant rice in a colander under cold running water, then add to the saucepan of simmering stock.

Simmer for 10–12 minutes or until the rice is tender and has absorbed the stock.

While the rice is cooking, heat the broiler to high. Line the broiler rack with foil and place the shrimp skewers on it in a single layer. Broil for 5 minutes until the shrimp turn pink, turning the skewers over halfway.

Stir the cilantro and chopped green chile into the coconut rice, and serve with the shrimp skewers.

Mussel and shrimp fritters

A popular street food in Bangkok, these fritters can be bought from road-side vendors who cook them fresh for customers. Use large mussels such as greenlip, and be sure to heat the oil to the correct temperature before you fry.

To make the fritters, sift the all-purpose flour and the baking powder into a mixing bowl. Make a well in the center, pour in half the beer, and stir until mixed well. Gradually whisk in the rest of the beer to make a smooth batter. Set aside to stand for 1 hour.

Dust the mussels and shrimp lightly in flour, and heat the oil to 350°F for deep-frying.

To make the dipping sauce, stir the ingredients together in a small bowl until the sugar dissolves.

Add a few mussels and shrimp to the batter, lift them out with tongs or a fork, and allow the excess batter to run back into the bowl. Add them to the hot oil and deep-fry for 2–3 minutes or until they are golden and crisp.

Drain the mussels and shrimp on paper towel and fry the rest in batches in the same way. Serve the fritters hot with the dipping sauce.

Ingredients

For the fritters:
8 oz all-purpose flour, plus extra to dust
½ tsp baking powder
8 fl. oz light beer
12 large mussels, such as greenlip
12 large raw shrimp, peeled
Peanut oil for deep-frying

For the dipping sauce:
2 tbsp fish sauce
2 tbsp lime juice
½ tsp sweet chilli sauce (see page 180)
1 tsp superfine sugar

Serves 4

Spicy seafood salad with sea bass

Ingredients

5 oz sea bass, cleaned, gutted, and thinly
   sliced into strips
5 oz large shrimp, shelled
5 oz squid, body and tentacles, cleaned,
   gutted, and sliced into ¾-in strips
7 fresh small green chiles
5 garlic cloves
2 coriander roots
2 tbsp fish sauce
½ tsp sugar
2 tbsp lime or lemon juice
4 scallions, sliced into ¼-in pieces
4 oz onion, thinly sliced
2 oz celery leaves and stalks, sliced

Serves 6

*T*he Thai version of a seafood salad is a flavorful assembly of
different ingredients quite unlike those featured in western
salads. Most are extremely spicy. This dish combines three of the
basic flavors: spicy, sour, and salty.

Cook the fish, shrimp, and squid separately in salted water for about 2–3 minutes each,
and then drain.

Pound the chiles, garlic, coriander root, fish sauce, and sugar together with a mortar
and pestle or in a food processor until finely blended.

Place this mixture in a bowl and mix in the lemon juice, scallions, onion, and celery. Stir
in the fish and seafood and mix well. Serve immediately.

Lime-dressed shrimp salad

*C*hoose green, unripe mangoes for this salad because ripe, golden-fleshed ones will be too sweet and have too soft a texture.

For the dressing, mix the ingredients together until the sugar dissolves. Set aside.

To make the salad, heat the sunflower oil in a wok and stir-fry the tiger shrimp for 1–2 minutes until they turn pink. Transfer to a bowl and pour over the dressing, stirring so all the shrimp are coated. Leave to cool.

Arrange the salad leaves, mango, red bell pepper, and cucumber on a serving dish and spoon the shrimp and dressing over the top.

Serve with lime wedges to squeeze over.

Ingredients

For the dressing:
5 tbsp sunflower oil
Juice of 2 limes
2 tbsp light soy sauce
½ tsp superfine sugar

For the salad:
1 tbsp sunflower oil
1 lb 2 oz raw tiger shrimp, peeled
4 oz mixed salad leaves (oriental or red stalk leaves)
1 green mango, peeled and flesh cut into fine sticks
½ red bell pepper, seeded and cut into fine sticks
2 oz cucumber, cut into fine sticks
Lime wedges for garnish

Serves 4

Steamed jumbo shrimp with lemongrass

Ingredients

1 lb raw jumbo shrimp
1 stalk of lemongrass,
   quartered lengthwise
8 scallions, trimmed and sliced
2 tbsp coarsely chopped fresh cilantro leaves
1 red chile, seeded and thinly sliced

For the sauce:
2 tbsp fish sauce
1 tsp superfine sugar
2 tbsp light soy sauce
½ lemongrass stalk, thinly sliced

Serves 4

A light aromatic dish that will appeal to anyone counting their calories. Skinless chicken breasts can also be cooked using the same method below.

Peel the shrimp and cut down the back of each one to remove the dark thread running down its length.

Place the lemongrass in a steamer and arrange the shrimp, scallions, cilantro, and red chile on top. Cover and steam over a saucepan of boiling water for 5 minutes or until the shrimp turn pink.

To make the sauce, mix together the fish sauce, superfine sugar, light soy sauce, and lemongrass until the sugar dissolves.

Lift the shrimp, scallions, cilantro, and red chile from the steamer and discard the lemongrass. Serve while still hot with the sauce spooned over.

Yellow chicken curry

*P*erhaps the least known internationally of Thailand's three color-coded curries—the others being green curry (see page 150) and red curry (see page 159)—this Indian-influenced recipe is very popular in the country's southern region.

Pound all the curry paste ingredients together with a mortar and pestle or in a blender until a fine paste is formed.

Fry the shallots until light brown and set aside.

Heat ½ pint of the coconut milk in a wok or pan, add the curry paste, and cook for 5 minutes. Add the rest of the coconut milk, bring to a boil, add the chicken and cook until tender, about 10 minutes.

Add the potato and salt, and cook until the potatoes are done, about 10 minutes. Pour into bowls, sprinkle with the fried shallots, and garnish with a sprig of kaffir lime. Serve accompanied by ajaad salad (see page 177), sliced pickled ginger, and steamed rice.

Ingredients

For the yellow curry paste:
2–3 yellow chiles, chopped
10 small garlic cloves, chopped
½ stalk of lemongrass, sliced
½ tbsp shallots, sliced
2 tsp chili powder
1 tsp sliced root ginger
1 tsp galangal, sliced
1 tsp shrimp paste (kapi)
1 tsp salt
½ tsp coriander seeds
½ tsp fennel seeds
½ tsp turmeric

For the curry:
3 tbsp sliced shallots
2½ pints thin coconut milk
1 lb chicken, cut into medium-sized pieces
7 oz potatoes, peeled and cut into
    ½-in cubes
2 tsp salt
Sprig of kaffir lime

Serves 6

Coconut beef curry

Ingredients

2 tbsp red curry paste (see page 156)

2 fl. oz peanut or corn oil

11 oz beef sirloin, cut into 1 x ¾ x ¼-in slices

1½ pints thin coconut milk

1 tbsp fish sauce

2 tsp sugar

2 fresh red chiles, sliced

2 kaffir lime leaves, sliced finely

3 oz Thai basil leaves

Serves 8

*D*espite the addition of coconut milk, this is still one of the driest of all Thai curries, and it is usually quite fiery. If you want to make it less spicy, simply reduce the number of chiles.

Heat the oil in a pan or wok and fry the curry paste for 3–4 minutes. Add the beef and fry for a further 2 minutes, then add the coconut milk and boil until the beef is tender, which should take about 15 minutes.

Add the fish sauce, sugar, and chile. Remove from the heat, transfer to a serving plate and sprinkle with the lime leaves and basil.

Serve in bowls accompanied by steamed rice, pickled vegetables, salted eggs, and sun-dried beef.

Southern chile curry with red and green chiles

As with most of the region's nam priks (spiced dishes), this thick, spicy southern curry is intended to be eaten with plain rice. Don't be fooled by its seeming simplicity; it is both tasty and satisfying, not to mention fairly fiery.

To make the chile paste, pound all the ingredients together finely with a mortar and pestle or in a food processor.

Boil the water in a pan or wok, add the chile paste and boil briefly before adding the pork, fish sauce, curry powder, and lime leaf.

Boil again for 10 minutes before transferring to four serving bowls. Serve accompanied by steamed rice.

Ingredients

For the chile paste:

8–10 small, dried green and red chiles, chopped

6 white peppercorns

2 tbsp shallots, sliced

1 tbsp sliced garlic

1 tsp sliced galangal

1 tsp shrimp paste (kapi)

¼ stalk of lemongrass, sliced

1½ pints water

8 oz pork loin, cut into 1¼ x ¾ x ¼-in pieces

3 tbsp fish sauce

1 tsp curry powder

3 kaffir lime leaves, torn into quarters

Serves 4

Whole steamed spiced chicken with a coconut sauce

Ingredients

3 lb oven-ready chicken
1 large lemon, halved
2 tsp grated fresh ginger
1 large red chile, finely chopped
2 garlic cloves, peeled and crushed
2 tsp finely chopped lemongrass
Juice of 1 medium lime
1 tbsp finely chopped fresh cilantro
Salt and freshly ground black pepper
½ tsp Thai spice powder (chili powder, dried
   garlic, ginger, ground coriander, ground
   cinnamon, ground cumin, star anise, and
   garlic powder)
2 tbsp vegetable oil
¼ pint dry white wine
Kaffir lime leaves

For the sauce:
¼ pint coconut milk
¼ pint chicken stock

Serves 4

*S*teaming a whole chicken is the perfect way to obtain a really succulent result, and it helps the meat to take on the wonderful Thai flavorings. If lime leaves are unavailable, use large mint or basil leaves. Cooks in Thailand blend their own spice mixes from ingredients bought at the local market. It is, however, possible to buy pre-blended mixtures of Thai spices at specialist southeast Asian food stores.

Wash the chicken inside and out, and pat dry. Place the halved lemon inside the cavity and transfer to a deep glass dish.

Mix the remaining ingredients together (except for the lime leaves) and pour over the chicken. Cover tightly and leave to marinate for at least 2 hours, turning occasionally.

Prepare the steamer, lining the base of the upper tier with the lime leaves. Remove the chicken from the dish, reserving the marinade, and place on top of the lime leaves. Cover and steam for 1–1¼ hours until cooked through.

Meanwhile, heat the marinade in a small saucepan with the stock and coconut milk. Serve with the chicken and steamed, fragrant rice (see page 128).

LEFT: A jungle path shaded by coconut groves on Koh Samui, an island of the southeast coast of Thailand.

Fried flat beans with pork

*Y*ou can use fresh lima beans as a substitute for the sator beans, but really the basis for this quintessentially southern dish is the strange flavor of the real thing. The recipe is included here for authenticity and just in case you are able to find the real sator beans in a Thai delicatessen or greengrocer. They are known by various other names, including petai beans, yongchak, and the rather unappealing sounding stinky beans.

Pound the chiles and garlic together with a mortar and pestle or whizz in a food processor to a fine paste. Mix with the shrimp paste.

Heat the oil in a pan or wok. Add the chile–garlic mixture, then add the pork and stir-fry for 3 minutes. Add the beans and all the remaining ingredients, plus 3 tablespoons of water if using lima beans, then fry until the beans are cooked. After about 10 minutes they should be quite firm.

Serve accompanied by rice.

Ingredients

3 fresh yellow or green chiles, chopped
1 tbsp chopped garlic
½ tsp shrimp paste (kapi)
2 tbsp peanut or corn oil
5 oz pork loin (or chicken or shrimp), cut into thin strips
1 lb fresh sator or lima beans
½ tsp fish sauce
½ tsp sugar
½ tsp lime or lemon juice

Serves 4

Fried rice-stick noodles with coconut sauce

Ingredients

10 oz dried rice-stick noodles
3 tbsp vegetable oil
2 cloves garlic, finely chopped
3 shallots, chopped
14 oz rump steak, thinly sliced
16 canned or fresh baby corn, cut diagonally
4 scallions, chopped
10 oz bean sprouts
14 fl. oz canned coconut milk
2 tsp jaggery (or soft brown sugar)
4 tbsp fish sauce
3 tbsp freshly squeezed lemon juice
1 tbsp red curry paste (see page 156)
Cilantro leaves, to garnish

Serves 4

*T*he coconut and its parent palm have a hallowed place in the Thai psyche, and nowhere more so than in the southern region where they grow in abundance. The coconut itself has a wide variety of culinary uses, while the palm is employed to make furniture, toys, and musical instruments. Canned coconut milk varies in its consistency depending on the brand. A thicker product produces the richest, smoothest flavor. Remember to shake the can well before opening.

Soak the noodles in warm water for 2–5 minutes, or follow the instructions on the package. Rinse and drain.

Heat the oil in a wok or skillet, then stir-fry the garlic and shallots for 30 seconds. Add the beef and stir-fry for about 3 minutes, before adding the baby corn, scallions, and bean sprouts.

Add the coconut milk, sugar, fish sauce, lemon juice, and curry paste, and stir well until the sauce is absorbed into the noodles.

Put the noodles onto four plates, sprinkle with cilantro leaves, and serve at once.

White noodle nests with fish

*T*he basis of this meal-in-a-bowl is a nest of long, thin rice noodles known as khanom chiin, which means "Chinese noodles." They are sold in markets thoughout the country and can be purchased in batches of up to a hundred.

Boil the green beans in water for 3–4 minutes, drain, then set aside.

Boil the fish in a small amount of water for 10 minutes. Remove with a slotted spoon and, when cool, finely chop.

Place the noodles in a pan and pour over boiling water to cover. Bring back to a boil and cook for 5 minutes, then drain. When cool, fold the noodles into four serving bowls.

In a pan, heat the coconut milk and chicken stock, then add the chile paste, fish, and fish sauce, and boil for 3 minutes. Remove from the heat and spoon over the noodles. Serve with small dishes of bean sprouts, beans, spinach, and Thai basil leaves.

Ingredients

6 oz chopped green beans
7 oz white fish fillets, skinned
8 oz dried vermicelli, soaked for
3–5 minutes
1½ pints coconut milk
1½ pints chicken stock
4 fl. oz red chile paste (see page 51)
3 tbsp fish sauce
4 oz bean sprouts, blanched
4 oz spinach, blanched
4 oz Thai basil leaves

Serves 4

Chile preserve

*T*here are probably as many recipes in Thailand for chile preserve as there are cooks, but the common ingredient in all of them is the large dried red chiles available from Thai food stores or other Asian food stores. Fresh chiles will not give the same intense flavor and color and their extra fluid will prevent the preserve from becoming thick and sticky.

Place the chiles in a bowl, cover with hot water, and leave to soak for 30 minutes. Drain, split open and remove the seeds.

Heat the oil for deep-frying in a wok and deep-fry the chiles for a couple of minutes until they are dark red. Drain on paper towel.

Remove all but 2 tablespoons of the oil and fry the red bell pepper and shallots for around 5 minutes. Add the garlic, fry for a further 2 minutes, and then stir in the tomatoes, chiles, and shrimp paste.

Lower the heat and simmer gently for 30 minutes. Cool a little, then purée in a food processor with the sugar and fish sauce.

Return the purée to the wok and cook it very gently for about 40 minutes until dark, caramelized, and jello-like in consistency, stirring regularly so it does not stick to the pan and burn.

Ingredients
½ oz large dried red chiles
Peanut oil for deep-frying
1 red bell pepper, seeded and chopped
4 purple shallots, peeled and chopped
2 cloves garlic, peeled and chopped
8 oz canned chopped tomatoes
1 tsp shrimp paste (kapi)
2 tbsp soft brown sugar
2 fl. oz fish sauce

Makes about 12 fl. oz

Crisp fried fish with chile preserve

*K*nown in Thailand as pra tod lard prik, this recipe works best if you add yeast to the batter mix as it will give the fish a wonderfully crisp, light coating that will not go soggy after frying. To activate the yeast effectively, it is important to stir it thoroughly into the flour before adding the liquid. The recipe can be prepared with any firm white fish. If using a flat fish, such as sole or flounder, cut the fillets into fairly wide strips and reduce the frying time to 2–3 minutes.

Sprinkle the yeast and sugar over the flour in a bowl and stir well. Add the water and mix with a wooden spoon to make a smooth batter. Cover and leave for 1 hour until frothy.

Heat the oil for deep-frying in a wok or large saucepan to 375°F. Stir the fresh cilantro into the batter.

Coast the fish pieces in the seasoned flour and dip into the batter until coated.

Fry a few pieces at a time in the hot oil for about 5 minutes or until golden brown and crisp. Drain on paper towel and keep warm while you fry the rest.

Serve the fish with a little of the chile preserve, garnished with wedges of lime for squeezing over the fish.

Ingredients

¼ oz dry yeast

Pinch of sugar

6 oz all-purpose flour, plus extra seasoned
    flour to coat the fish

5 fl. oz tepid water

Peanut or vegetable oil for deep-frying

1 tbsp chopped fresh cilantro

1¼ lb firm white fish fillets, such as monkfish,
    sea bass, or cod, cut into 2-in pieces

Chile preserve (see opposite)

Lime wedges

Serves 4

Salmon steaks in peanut and chile sauce

Ingredients

4 salmon steaks, about 6 oz each
1 small onion, sliced
2 bay leaves
Few sprigs of parsley
4–5 peppercorns
4 fl. oz dry white wine
1 tbsp white wine vinegar
2 fl. oz water

Fo the sauce:
2 tbsp olive oil
1 garlic clove, crushed
1-in piece root ginger, peeled and grated
4 oz raw peanuts, shelled
2 red chiles, seeded and sliced
2 tsp soft dark brown sugar
8 fl. oz vegetable stock
1 tbsp lemon juice
Lemon slices to garnish

Serves 4

*T*his recipe features three of the most popular ingredients in southern Thai cooking: fresh fish, peanuts, and fiery hot chiles.

Wipe the salmon and reserve. Place the onion, bay leaves, parsley, peppercorns, wine, and vinegar in a frying pan. Add the water and leave to boil. Reduce the heat and simmer for 10 minutes. Strain and reserve the liquor until ready to cook the fish.

Heat the oil for the sauce in the frying pan and fry the garlic and ginger for 2 minutes. Add the peanuts and fry gently for 10 minutes, or until golden.

Put the peanuts, garlic, ginger, and oil, along with the remaining sauce ingredients, in a food processor. Blend to a purée, then return to the cleaned pan and simmer for 8–10 minutes, or until reduced slightly. Keep warm while cooking the fish.

When ready to cook the fish, reheat the reserved liquor in the frying pan and add the fish. Bring to a boil, then cover and reduce the heat to a very gently simmer. Cook for 3–4 minutes, or until the fish is cooked. Drain and arrange on serving plates and spoon over a little sauce. Garnish with lemon slices.

LEFT: Squid caught in Chumpon, southern Thailand, hanging out to dry above a sheltered bay.

Coconut custard

*I*n Thailand, coconut milk is often used to make a sweet, creamy custard known as sankhaya, which is cooked in a double boiler and then a steamer to prevent bubbles forming in the custard. Canned Thai coconut milk is the right consistency for the recipe but because cream tends to settle on the top, the milk needs a good stir or a quick whizz in a food processor to restore its smooth texture. Take care not to allow the custard to boil or it will curdle. If this does happen, remove the saucepan from the heat and strain, or process the custard in a food processor until smooth again.

Ingredients
2 large eggs, lightly beaten
2 oz white sugar
8 fl. oz thick canned coconut milk
Few drops of vanilla extract

Makes 4

Whisk the eggs and sugar together until creamy, then stir in the coconut milk until evenly blended.

Strain into a double boiler set over a pan of boiling water and cook gently, stirring constantly, until the mixture coats the back of a wooden spoon. Stir in the vanilla and pour the custard into four small bowls or ramekins. Cover lightly with foil and steam over just-simmering water for 15 minutes or until the custards are just set. Let cool.

Coconut custard with spiced fruit salad

Most meals in Thailand end not with a dessert but with a platter of the many luscious fruits that grow all over the country. In this recipe, the coconut custard is served with a fresh fruit salad lightly spiced with cinnamon, star anise, and cloves. If you want to spice things up a bit more, add a little grated fresh root ginger, bruised lemongrass stalk, or split vanilla bean to the pineapple juice. If rambutans are not available, lychees can be substituted. You might also like to dust the top of the custards with a little ground cinnamon before serving.

Place the pineapple juice in a small pan, add the star anise, cinnamon, and cloves and bring to a simmering point. Remove from the heat and set aside to cool.

Pile the prepared fruit in a serving bowl and pour the spiced juice over it. Chill until ready to serve.

Spoon the fruit salad onto serving plates, with the small bowls of custard on the side.

Ingredients

10 fl. oz pineapple juice
2 star anise
1 cinnamon stick, broken into short lengths
4 cloves
1 mango, peeled and sliced
½ papaya, peeled, seeded, and chopped
1 slice pineapple, cut into small pieces
4 rambutans, peeled, pitted, and halved
1 star fruit, sliced
Seeds from ½ pomegranate
4 coconut custards (see opposite)

Serves 4

Banana and pineapple fritters in coconut batter

*T*his is a popular street snack in Thailand where roadside chefs toss the crisp fritters in woks of crackling oil. If using canned pineapple, drain it well and blot away any juice with a paper towel before coating with the batter. Use slightly under-ripe bananas so they do not become too soft when cooked.

Sift the flour and ginger into a bowl and stir in the superfine sugar. Make a well in the center of the dry ingredients and pour in the coconut milk. Whisk to make a smooth batter, and then set aside for 30 minutes.

Heat the peanut oil to 350°F for deep-frying.

Dust the banana and pineapple pieces with flour, dip in the batter until coated, and deep-fry in batches for 2–3 minutes until golden and crisp. Drain on paper towel and serve scattered with desiccated coconut, or coconut ice cream.

Ingredients

8 oz all-purpose flour, plus extra for dusting
½ tsp ground ginger
2 oz superfine sugar
8 fl. oz coconut milk
Peanut oil for deep-frying
2 bananas, peeled and
   cut into 2-in lengths
2 pineapple rings, quartered
Shredded young coconut
   or desiccated coconut

Serves 4

Coconut jello

Ingredients
4 sheets of leaf gelatin
6 fl. oz coconut milk
6 fl. oz water
2 oz superfine sugar
2 oz young coconut, grated
Toasted fresh or desiccated coconut

Makes 20

*S*erve this cut up into small pieces as it is rich and very sweet. Be sure to stir the gelatin until it is fully dissolved to give the jello a lovely smooth texture.

Soak the gelatin leaves in a little cold water for 5 minutes to soften. Remove and squeeze them out.

Heat the coconut milk, water, and sugar in a pan until almost boiling, add the gelatin leaves, and stir until dissolved.

Add the grated coconut, pour into a shallow tray lined with plastic wrap, and allow to cool. Chill until set.

Serve the jelly cut into small triangles, squares, or flower shapes using a fluted cutter, and scatter with toasted fresh or desiccated coconut.

Index

Picture credits

The images in this book are used with the permission of the copyright holders stated below. (Images are listed by page number.) All other illustrations and pictures are © Quintet Publishing Limited. While every effort has been made to credit contributors, Quintet would like to apologize should there have been any omissions or errors and would be pleased to make the appropriate correction for future editions of the book.